LIFE UNDER THE
PHARAOHS

LIFE UNDER THE
PHARAOHS

LEONARD COTTRELL

SUTTON PUBLISHING

This book was first published in 1955 by
Evans Brothers Limited

This edition first published in 2004 by
Sutton Publishing Limited · Phoenix Mill
Thrupp · Stroud · Gloucestershire · GL5 2BU

British Library Cataloguing in Publication Data
A catalogue record for this book is aviable from the British
Library.

ISBN 0 7509 3723 8

The publishers regret that it was not possible to reproduce the
original illustrations in this edition.

Prrinted and bound in Great Britain by
J.H. Haynes & Co. Ltd, Sparkford.

To
SIR ALAN GARDINER

in
appreciation of a
valued friendship

CONTENTS

LIFE UNDER THE
PHARAOHS

INTRODUCTION

A FEW years ago I wrote a book called *The Lost Pharaohs* which began with the words, "This is a book by an amateur for the amateur". It was an attempt to provide an accurate but simply written and readable introduction to the study of Ancient Egypt. The present work, which is by way of a sequel to the first, falls into a similar category, though its aim is somewhat different. *The Lost Pharaohs* begins with an outline of Egyptian history, from pre-Dynastic times (i.e. before 3100 B.C.) to the coming of the Romans, and goes on to describe the beginnings of Egyptology as a science, with the decipherment of the hieroglyphs, and the gradual unfolding of the Ancient Egyptian civilisation through the successive discoveries of great archaeologists, from Mariette to Montet.

After the book was published a number of readers were kind enough to write to me suggesting a further volume dealing more fully than was possible in *The Lost Pharaohs* with the *everyday* life of the Ancient Egyptians. I put the idea on one side at first, partly because there already exist a number of excellent and scholarly works on this highly specialised subject, but chiefly because I was writing a book on ancient Crete and had temporarily transferred my allegiance from Pharaoh to King Minos.

Then, last year, I went back to Egypt. Although I was there on business which was far removed from Egyptology, I had the opportunity of meeting some of my old friends among the Egyptian archaeologists, and revisiting some of the sites I had known seven years ago. And once I was out of Cairo, when I saw again the long brown ridge of the Pyramid plateau, when I stood with my friend Zakaria

Goneim beside the Step Pyramid at Sakkara and gazed out across that wonderful green valley, all the old fascination returned; my re-kindled enthusiasm burned brighter than ever and I knew that I had to write another book on Egypt. I went again to Luxor, walked again in the Valley of the Tombs of the Kings, talked far into the night with Labib Habachi, the Chief Inspector of Antiquities at Luxor, and with him and other friends discussed the latest developments in Egyptian excavation and research. I also revisited the Egyptian Museum in Cairo, and through the courtesy of Dr. Mustapha Amer, the Director of the Sérvice des Antiquités, was able to see and photograph the royal mummies which are not on public exhibition.

But this time I did not look only at the ancient monuments. I was able to spend a little time as a guest in Egyptian villages where fragments of the ancient Egyptian language still survive, to meet and talk with the *fellahin*, who, despite their Arabic veneer, are the lineal descendants of the Ancient Egyptians, and to watch ceremonies and customs for which one can find parallels in the days of the Pharaohs. In particular I am grateful to Mr. Youssef el Afifi, Director of the Unesco Centre at Sirs-el-Layan, who has spent a lifetime studying the country people, and to Dr. George Sobhy, an Egyptian surgeon who is also an Egyptologist, and who, besides being an authority on the Coptic language, has done some remarkable research upon the survival of the ancient language and folk-customs, particularly in the field of medicine.

However, there remained the problem of what form this book should take. A number of specialised works have been written, by professional Egyptologists, on the everyday life of the Ancient Egyptians, though many of these are now out of print. I am not a specialist, and I would not be so presumptuous as to attempt to write a comprehensive textbook on Egyptian life and culture, for which task others are far better qualified than I. In any case, I must say frankly that not every aspect of this ancient civilisation attracts me equally, and readers who want, for example, a fully-documented account of Egyptian law and administration or military organisation can find these dealt with in the more specialised works to which I have referred, and which are given in the Bibliography at the end of this book.

Broadly speaking, the book deals with the daily life of the Pharaoh's people, the houses they lived in, the dress they wore, how they amused themselves, with chapters on such subjects as the life of women and children, of the soldier, the scribe, the doctor, the craftsman, and the great administrator. But in choosing my subjects I have been guided mainly by my own preferences and enthusiasms, for only in this way could I give the book life. Therefore, as far as possible, each chapter has been linked with some scene or object, the sculptured head of a woman, a child's toy, a painted scene in an Egyptian tomb, a poem, a story, or even some modern parallel with the life of the ancient people which I have observed among the modern *fellahin*; these personal memories, of things which have moved or intrigued me, they provide the springboards of my various chapters.

Even so, it seemed to me that a book about people *en masse* stood in grave danger of boring the general reader. I therefore went a step further and between each chapter of factual information I inserted other chapters in which I have tried to create a group of characters, the Vizier Rekhmire, and his family and friends, and to set them in motion against their native surroundings. Although some (though not all) of their activities are fictitious, all could have happened; the Vizier and his wife Meryet were real persons and their tomb still remains in the Theban Necropolis. Readers who are curious to know how much is real and how much imagined will find the answers in the Appendix "Fact or Fiction?"

Many years ago I came across a passage in a book by Arthur Weigall, an Egyptologist who never wrote a dull line, and which I will take the liberty of quoting because it sums up my own approach to the study of the ancient world:

"A man has no more right to think of the people of old as dust than he has to think of his contemporaries as lumps of meat. The true archaeologist does not take pleasure in skeletons as skeletons, for his whole effort is to cover them decently with flesh and skin once more, and to put some thoughts back in the empty skulls. Nor does he delight in ruined buildings because they are ruined buildings; rather he deplores that they are ruined. . . . In fact, the archaeologist is so enamoured of life that he would raise all the dead from their graves. He will not have it that the men of old are dust; he would bring them forth to share with him the sunlight which he finds so precious. He is such an enemy of Death and Decay that he would rob them of their harvest; and for every life that the foe has claimed he would raise up, if he could, a memory that would continue to live."

LEONARD COTTRELL.

CHAPTER I

THE LAND, THE PEOPLE AND THEIR GODS

It is an old truism that a people's character is formed by the land and the climate in which it lives. If this is true of people like the English, who have occupied their country for less than 1,500 years, or the Americans, who have settled in their vast continent for only a few generations, how much more true it is of the Egyptians, who have lived in their narrow, desert-bounded valley for more than 6,000 years! Also, whereas other countries have changed and developed over the centuries, losing much of their original character, Egypt has not. The same conditions which governed the lives of the millions who lived under the Pharaohs still largely apply to-day. Therefore, before one can attempt to describe the people it is necessary to present a picture, however sketchy, of this extraordinary country, the like of which exists nowhere else in the world.

Not long ago I was lying in my berth in a *wagon-lit* which was trundling through the night along the 400-odd miles which separate Luxor, in Upper Egypt, from Cairo. A few days before I had travelled up to Luxor by day, a journey which took ten hours; the view from the train windows was a monotonous, never-ending panorama of cotton-fields, sugar-plantations, mud-brick villages, palm trees, always with the brown desert hills to right and left, sometimes coming close, at other times retreating into the distance, but never absent from view. It was like watching a travel film endlessly repeated.

But there is something about the night journey which always stirs my imagination—I do not quite know why. The train rumbles and rocks, the rapid puffing of the

locomotive roars in the ventilators, and as one lies com-
fortably in one's bunk, pictures form in the mind.

I imagined some watcher from the skies, a sky-deity,
looking down on this green serpent, the Nile Valley,
coiling through the desert waste for 600 miles and more,
never more than a few miles wide and often less than a
mile in width. On the west stretches an endless waste of
sand and rock—the Sahara. On the other side the Arabian
Desert rolls eastward for hundreds of miles until it reaches
the Red Sea. There is a full moon and my sky-god would
see the great river shining like pale silver. Here and there
he would see a sprinkling of lights along the banks—towns
like Keneh, and Asuit, and Ballana. But he would not see
the hundreds of unlighted villages where the millions of
fellahin sleep the sleep of exhaustion, huddled in their
mud-brick villages, until the sun calls them out to the flat
fields to continue their eternal labours.

To how many millions of human souls has this green
snake given birth during the past hundred centuries?
As an Immortal, my sky-god would remember the time
when the green gash in the desert was known only to
animals, birds and reptiles; when lions and hyenas, cheetahs
and wolves roamed the desert fringes, and hippopotami
splashed in the water; when huge flocks of geese rose above
the papyrus marshes in clouds, before man was known in
the valley.

My god would have seen how, century after century,
the jungle gave way to cultivation. He would have seen,
for the first time on this planet, ordered cities developing,
surrounded by fields, threaded by roads and canals, while
the rest of the human race, or most of it, still wandered
from hunting-ground to hunting-ground, barbarians whose
only skill was in killing animals to maintain a mere existence.

Later, some 4,500 years ago, he would have seen the
Pyramids rising, sprinkled like a child's building-blocks
along thirty miles of the western bank, the eternal homes

of kings who wanted to be gods. He would see the great city of Memphis with its palaces, temples and gardens, and other towns scattered along the valley from the Delta to the Nubian frontier. Fifteen centuries later he would have seen Thebes, the Imperial City, rising stately under the hacked ridges of the Theban hills. If he had peered low enough he might have caught the gleam of the Pharaoh's golden war-chariots and the dust rising behind the columns of his marching soldiers, moving southward to punish the Nubians, or north-eastwards to do battle with the Hittites.

He would remember the Cretan ships moving up the Nile to Thebes, bearing gifts for the Pharaoh, and later, ships of a different sort, manned by the fierce men of Macedonia, led by the generals of Alexander the Great. He saw the coming of the Romans, watched Hadrian's legionaries camping beside the colossi of Memnon at Luxor, where the soldiers pottered about among the 1,000-year-old tombs, and scrawled initials on the walls just as the tourists of the nineteenth century used to do.

The armies of the Prophet with their horses and banners, the Turks, the armies of Napoleon, Nelson's fleet at Aboukir, Gordon marching south to his death at Khartoum, the flash of the guns before Alamein . . . all these he would have seen. And now he would mark a train crawling northward beside the winding river, a red glow followed by a string of lights.

I think that is why this journey, which I have made several times, will never lose its fascination for me. When you take the train from Luxor to Cairo you travel in ten hours through more than half the history of mankind.

*   *   *

There, then, is the land; narrow, constricted, hemmed in by its inhospitable deserts, but fertilised everlastingly by the mud brought down each year by the flooding Nile. For more than 3,000 years before the birth of Christ the oldest civilisation on earth flourished in that narrow valley. The Pyramids, the tombs, the temples and obelisks speak of the power of its kings, the mysteries of its religion, and the richness of its culture. Also, because of their passionate love of this life and their anxiety that it should continue in the after-world, the wealthier Egyptians have left in their tombs paintings and sculptures which vividly illustrate the occupations, pursuits and pleasures which they enjoyed in this life, and which they ardently wished should continue in the next.

They have also left us many examples of their furniture, their dress, models of their houses, their weapons of war, their boats, their games and amusements, and documents which range from official histories, religious texts and business transactions to school exercises, poems and romances.

And yet for all this the Egyptians remain for most of us a mysterious race of people. This is partly due to the fact that until about 120 years ago, when the hieroglyphs began to be deciphered, they *were* mysterious, a people who had left monuments, sculptures and paintings, but whose language was unknown. It is true that classical historians and travellers like Herodotus, Pliny, and Diodorus Siculus had left records of their travels in Egypt, but these tended only to strengthen the legend, for if the religious and other customs which Herodotus described seemed strange to him, how much more strange must they appear to the nineteenth-century historians? And even when the hieroglyphs were imperfectly translated the bulk of records and inscriptions seemed to be concerned, not with warm-blooded human beings like ourselves, who made love, bore and brought up children, followed careers, enjoyed sports and pastimes, but of a morbid, melancholy race, perpetually obsessed with death, whose religion seemed a hotch-potch of magic and superstition, of animal-headed gods and monsters which, unlike the Greek gods and goddesses, hadn't even the merit of possessing human qualities like our own.

This, as we know now, was a libel on the Ancient Egyptians, who, like their modern descendants, seem to have been an extremely cheerful, life-loving people, but it is not difficult to see how they acquired their undeserved reputation for gloom and mystery. First, they had a fervent hope for an after-life, which in the case of them all except their god-kings was to be very like this one. In order to enjoy this after-life, they thought it necessary to build for themselves, if they could afford it, an "Eternal Habitation"— a tomb which would last for eternity—and to place within it, either in actuality or representation, the articles they would need to make life comfortable and happy, their clothes, their furniture, and household goods, the boats in which they would travel along the heavenly Nile, their hunting weapons with which they would spear fish or catch wildfowl, and representations, either statues or wall-reliefs, of the servants who would minister to them after death as they had in life. It is this materialistic attitude to death which has left us the legacy of beautiful or curious objects which are scattered throughout the museums of the world.

Second, whereas their homes were built of perishable material, usually mud-brick and timber, which have disappeared, their tombs were built to last for ever, and have therefore survived. The same is true of the great temples which were the homes of their gods. The colossal temple of Amun at Karnak, with its 70-foot drum columns and massive pylons, remains to awe and astonish us, but the palaces of the Kings, the mansions of the nobles with their courts and gardens, and the million dwellings of lesser men, have largely disappeared. The result is that when we visit Egypt we see either tombs or religious buildings, or if we visit our local museum we shall find that most of the objects on view have either a religious or funerary significance. It is as if a visitor coming to Britain or America 3,000 years hence should find nothing remaining but

churches and cemeteries. Such a visitor might be excused for
imagining that we had spent most of our time in the worship
of God or the care of our dead, but he would be wrong.

Similarly with Egypt; the work of hundreds of scholars,
philologists poring over papyri, excavators discovering
tombs, or sifting among the scanty remains of ancient
towns, students laboriously copying and photographing
tomb-paintings, have produced a wealth of human material
which proves that the Ancient Egyptians had other occupations and interests besides worshipping their gods or
preparing for the next world. It is from this material,
and from my own observations, that I hope to paint a
picture of ancient Egyptian life: in camps and courts, on
the farms, in the law-courts and temples, and not least in
the home. But there are certain difficulties and dangers of
which the reader should be warned in advance.

The first is a fairly obvious one: the fact that the period
of Egyptian history with which we are to deal covers over
3,000 years, a period three times as long as that which
separates us from Alfred the Great. One has only to reflect
on the changes which have occurred in English manners
and customs in half that time to understand the difficulty
of describing the life of a people over thirty centuries. To
take each phase of Egyptian history in turn and describe the
evolution of dress and furniture alone would require several
books of this size. However, the writer (and the reader)
can take comfort from the fact that the Ancient Egyptians
were a very conservative people, and although important
changes in dress and manners did take place over that
enormous period of time, certain basic elements did not
alter; even during the time of the Ptolemies, in the third
century B.C., art and architecture, dress and religious
observances bore, to the untutored eye, a very close
resemblance to those of the Pyramid-builders, who lived
more than 2,000 years earlier. Even to-day the pattern of
agricultural life in Egypt is not unlike what it was in

Pharaonic times. From the train which carried me to Luxor I saw peasants digging the furrows with hoes exactly like those shown on the shoulders of the *shawabti* figures,[1] and in a Delta village I examined primitive beehives of mud-brick, shaped like a drain-pipe, which the Ancient Egyptians also used. Even the musical instruments with which the *fellah* amuses himself in his few hours of leisure are like those depicted in the Theban tomb-paintings.

However, to avoid confusion, I shall be careful to state from which particular period of Egyptian history—the Old, Middle, or New Kingdoms—my illustrations are drawn, and for those who are not familiar with these main dynastic divisions there is a Dynastic table at the end of this book. For those who require more detailed information I would recommend that they read *The Lost Pharaohs*, to which this is a companion volume, or any of the standard textbooks recommended in the Bibliography.

The second difficulty, to which I drew attention above, is more subtle and dangerous. It is the danger that, because the Ancient Egyptians were human beings like ourselves, with the same passions, appetites, and failings, because they sat on chairs, slept on beds, sent their children to school or their sons into the Army, we may grow to think that they were more like us than they really were. True, human nature has changed remarkably little in 5,000 years, but, civilised though they undoubtedly were, the gap which separated the Egyptians from primitive beliefs was much narrower than it is with us. Their religion, though it had an ethical content, was full of animism and magic, survivals of the not-so-distant days before the first civilisation grew up along the Nile Valley. "In that world the savage ancestors of the Ancient Egyptians lived in fear, surrounded by hostile forces which had to be outwitted by magic or placated by blood-sacrifice."

[1] Funerary statuettes of servants left in Ancient Egyptian tombs to serve their masters in the after-world.

To say that their religion dominated their lives is probably
an exaggeration, but it certainly played a much more
important part in their daily lives than does the religion
of most Occidental peoples. Unless we recognise this,
unless we make the effort of imagination needed to enter
into their minds, we shall never understand them. Therefore, before I begin my "close-ups" of individual aspects
of Egyptian life I would like to sketch in this fundamental,
ever-present background of religious belief.

There is an excellent and recently-published book,
Before Philosophy, by Frankfort, Wilson, and Jacobsen,
which is a great help in understanding this background, and
I will take the liberty of quoting from it. After pointing out
the isolation of Ancient Egypt, with its high population
concentrated in the narrow valley of the Nile, the authors
say:

"The two features of isolation and semi-urban population
combine to make Egypt different from her neighbours. . . .

"The Egyptians are not subject to the great conservative control of the Arabian Desert. The deserts adjacent to Palestine are
potential breeding-grounds for fierce and puritanical elements in
the population of those countries. Egypt, with her agricultural
wealth and with her people living cheek by jowl, developed an
early sophistication, which expressed itself intellectually towards
catholicity and syncretism. Within Egypt the most divergent
concepts were tolerantly accepted and woven together into what
we moderns might regard as a clashing philosophical lack of
system, but which to the ancient was *inclusive*. The way of the
Semite, who held contact with the desert, was to cling fiercely to
tradition and resist innovations, which changed the purity and
simplicity of life. The way of the Egyptian was to accept innovations and incorporate them into his thought *without discarding
the old and outmoded*. [Our italics.] Old and new link blandly together like some surrealist picture of youth and age on a single
face."

Just how complex the religion was may be judged by the

fact that scholars have identified 2,000 separate deities in the
Egyptian pantheon. Before Egypt became a unified state
at the beginning of the First Dynasty (3200 B.C.) the Nile
Valley was inhabited by hundreds of separate tribes, each
of which had its own local deity. Of these, some were
deified chieftains, some were animals, reptiles or birds,
others were tree-spirits or totems. After unification, which
was first accomplished by King Menes, the god of the
town or province from which the ruling family came
usually became the chief or "state" god. For instance, in
the Old Kingdom (2780-2100 B.C.)—the age of the
Pyramid builders, the state god was the solar deity Re, whose
worship centred at Heliopolis, not far from the capital of
Memphis. Much later, when a Theban family ruled Egypt,
Amun, the god of Thebes, shared pride of place with Re;
in fact the two became identified under the name Amun-Re,
"King of the Gods". But this did not mean that the
hundreds of local godlings were discarded. They continued
to be worshipped in their districts, and were absorbed by
the systematising priesthood in a complex theological
system which must have been almost as bewildering to the
ordinary Egyptian as it is to us.

In the Middle Kingdom (2100 to 1700 B.C.) the most
important religious development was the rise of the Osiris
cult which continued to be practised right down to the
Roman period, and which probably had more influence over
the mass of the people than Amun-Re. The following brief
account of the cult, which I quote from my earlier book,
may be useful in helping to understand the part which the
legend of Isis and Osiris played in the everyday life of the
Ancient Egyptians:

"Like most primitive peoples the ancestors of the Ancient
Egyptians had their folk-myths which explained the origin of the
world. They believed that in the beginning only the ocean
existed, and on this ocean appeared an egg (in some versions a
flower) from which was born the sun-god. He had four children,

Geb and Shu, Tefnut and Nut. Planting their feet on Geb, Shu and Tefnut raised their sister Nut to the heavens. Thus Geb became the earth, Shu and Tefnut the atmosphere, and Nut the sky. Geb and Nut had four children, Osiris and Isis, Nepthys and Seth. Osiris succeeded to the throne of his father and governed the world wisely and justly, aided by his sister Isis, whom he married. Seth, jealous of his brother's power, plotted to destroy him and eventually succeeded, afterwards cutting the body of Osiris into pieces which he buried in several parts of Egypt. The head was buried at Abydos. The faithful Isis recovered the scattered fragments of her husband's corpse, and with the aid of the jackal-god Anubis, who subsequently became the god of embalment, re-animated it. Though unable to return to his life on earth, Osiris passed to the Underworld, where he became the god of the dead and later the judge of souls. Isis bore a son, Horus, who afterwards took revenge on his uncle, Seth, defeating the usurper in battle and winning back his father's throne.

"The legend became the most popular of all Egyptian folk-myths. It never lost its hold on the people, because of its human appeal, Isis becoming the type of loyal wife and mother, Horus the ideal son. In the Middle Kingdom it developed into the leading cult, and Abydos, supposed burial-place of the head of Osiris, became a place of pilgrimage. Every year thousands flocked to Abydos to watch a dramatic re-enactment of scenes in the life of Osiris, and to follow the procession of the God's body to his supposed tomb. Abydos thus became one of the most sacred places in Egypt. Noble families sought burial there, and others, who could not afford a tomb, erected memorial tablets in the hope that the God of the Dead would remember their names. It was during the 'Middle Kingdom' that the conception of Osiris as a *judge of souls* became predominant, and for the first time the idea of accountability in the after-life for sins committed on earth began to take hold of the human mind."

Comparisons have been drawn between the Osiris cult and Christianity, and some of the resemblances are striking. Isis, the mother-goddess, is frequently shown with the infant Horus in her arms, as Mary is shown with the infant Jesus. Also Osiris was a god of resurrection, and in many tombs archaeologists have found wooden trays containing corn-seeds, cut out in the form of the god, the corn symbolising the renewal of life. Similarly, when a man died he became "an Osiris" and was represented in the tomb-paintings in the form of the mummified god.

Though the complexities of the higher Egyptian theology probably meant nothing to the mass of the people, and though they were only allowed in the precincts of the great temples of Amun-Re, the state god, it is important to remember that these and other lesser deities were woven into the lives of the common people. In every museum and antiquity shop in the world you will find tiny bronze and faience statuettes of Amun-Re, of Isis and Osiris, of Hathor, goddess of love and beauty, of fat little Bes, the god of music and dancing, and hundreds of others. These were the daily companions of the people, occupying the same honoured place in Egyptian homes as do the statuettes of Christ and His saints in millions of Christian homes to-day. Similarly, an Egyptian mother probably taught her children the stories of Isis, the good wife and mother, of Horus, the good son, and Seth, the wicked god, in much the same way that Christian mothers teach their children the stories of the Bible.

But there is an important difference, which it is well to remember if one is to avoid falling into the trap against which I gave warning earlier in this chapter: the error of too closely identifying the Ancient Egyptian mind with our own. It is not difficult to draw parallels between the Osiris cult and Christianity, because the former is the most spiritual of the Egyptian cults, and embodies moral attitudes which we can understand. Evil is punished and good triumphs; the wronged and suffering God is saved by his sister-wife, is restored to life and becomes the judge of souls, while his son wreaks vengeance on the evildoer. But when we come to consider the other deities the modern mind meets with difficulties.

I can best illustrate them by asking the reader to consider first the personalities of the Old and New Testaments; second, the Greek and Roman deities; and, third, a typical group of gods and goddesses of Ancient Egypt.

In the first example, all the people involved, save One, are human beings; some are prophets, divinely inspired, some are saints and martyrs, but all are undoubtedly human, even if some of them have spiritual qualities which transcend ours. In the second case we are dealing with supernatural beings, Zeus, the King of gods, Poseidon, the god of the ocean, Aphrodite, the goddess of love, Ares, the god of war, and so on. But though they are immortals endowed with superhuman powers they are still recognisably human; they have human forms and human frailties.

Now look at a typical frieze representing some of the deities of the Egyptian pantheon. Here is a god with the body of a man and the head of a jackal. Here is another with the head of a ram. Beside him stands a woman with the head of a lioness and not far away crouches a crocodile; but he is a god too; so is the cow which stands nearby, while the figure of the king crouches below, sucking milk from her udders. She is Hathor, who in one of her aspects is the Egyptian goddess of love.

It is this which baffles our modern Western minds. Here was a people whose buildings, statuary and paintings still astonish the world; a people which built the Pyramids and the Karnak Temple; they understood astronomy and were capable of precise geometrical calculation; they practised medicine and surgery; they had a highly organised civil administration; they conquered and administered an Empire which at one time stretched from the Sudan to the Euphrates; they developed an elaborate system of writing and had a reputation for wisdom which even the Greeks acknowledged. And yet these same people worshipped and mummified cats and snakes, and had as one of their principal gods a bull which, after being worshipped in life, was after death embalmed, adorned with gold like a king, and ceremonially buried in a huge rock-cut sepulchre specially made for the purpose. Nor were the Egyptians alone in this; the Minoans of Crete, the Assyrians and Babylonians, also highly developed peoples, practised animal cults as strange as this. And not only were animals worshipped; there were sacred stones, sacred trees, sacred pillars.

Here is the gulf which separates us from the men and women of those early civilisations; it is a gulf which, perhaps, can never be completely bridged, but with a little imagination and knowledge we can go a long way to meet them. The anthropologist who has studied the habits of primitive man in the modern world can help us. Here, for instance, is a useful thought from *Before Philosophy*, from which I have already quoted:

"The fundamental difference between the attitudes of modern and ancient man as regards the surrounding world is this; for modern, scientific man the phenomenal world is primarily an 'It'. For ancient—and also for primitive—man it is 'Thou'. . . . An object, an 'It' can always be scientifically related to other objects and appear as part of a group or series. In this manner science insists on seeing 'It'; hence science is able to comprehend objects and events as ruled by universal laws which make their behaviour under given circumstances predictable. 'Thou' has the unprecedented, unparalleled, and unpredictable character of an individual, a presence known only in so far as it reveals itself. . . . For these reasons there is justification for the aphorism of Crawley: 'Primitive man has only one mode of thought, one mode of expression, one part of speech—*the personal*.' This does not mean (as is often thought) that primitive man, in order to explain natural phenomena, imparts human characteristics to an inanimate world. *Primitive man simply does not know an inanimate world*. [Our italics.]

"For this very reason he does not 'personify' the inanimate phenomena nor does he fill an empty world with the ghosts of the dead, as 'animism' would have us believe. The world appears to primitive man neither inanimate nor empty but abundant with life; and life has individuality, in man or beast or plant, and in every phenomena which confronts man—the thunderclap—the sudden shower—the eerie unknown clearing in the wood, the stone which suddenly hurts him when he stumbles while on a hunting trip. Any phenomenon may at any time face him, not as 'It' but as 'Thou'."

The Ancient Egyptians, though a highly civilised people, were much nearer to primitive man than we are, and their attitude to their natural surroundings, to the animal world, and to what we now call "the forces of Nature" can best be understood within the framework of this "Thou" relationship. Then it is easier to understand why they deified animals. As Wilson says, "The falcon floating in the sky with no more apparent motive power than the sun; the jackal flitting ghostlike along the margin of the desert; the crocodile lurking lump-like on the mud-flats; or the powerful bull in whom was the seed of procreation. These beasts were forces going beyond the normality of the landscape; they were forces which transcended the minimal observed natures of animals. They therefore took on high relief in the scene and were believed to be vested with mysterious or inscrutable forces related to an extra-human world."

To put it in another way: before science showed mechanism which animates plants and animals, before man knew that animals, reptiles and birds were of a lower but kindred species to himself, *he could only judge them in relation to his own humanity*; what interested and awed him was the fact that they were so different from himself, and that they possessed powers and functions which he had not. The bird with its power of flight, the lion with its immense strength, the crocodile which lurked in the river and could take off a man's leg with a snap of its jaws, the snake with its secret, silent, furtive life, and the ibis with its dignified air of wisdom; he did not catch these animals and study them in zoos: he respected and revered them because they possessed super-human powers. And therefore, in time, the flying falcon became the one of the insignia of royalty, the crocodile an infernal monster which devoured guilty souls, the ibis became Thoth, the god of wisdom (and of writing) and the lion, as the Sphinx, symbolised kingly majesty.

Remember also that the Egyptian in his narrow valley lived far closer to animals than we do; crocodiles and hippopotami swarmed in the river, huge flocks of geese lived in the papyrus marshes, falcons hovered in the sky. If we bear these facts in mind we shall be able to understand better the mysterious, and to us sometimes grotesque aspects of the religion which was the ever-present background to the Egyptian's daily life.

CHAPTER II

REKHMIRE COMES HOME

My aim is to get as close as possible to the daily life of the Ancient Egyptians. I have said something about their land and the gods they worshipped. If this were a classified textbook, with each aspect of Egyptian life neatly tabulated under headings, this chapter would be headed "Law and Administration" or "How They were Governed". It is important that these matters should be understood, but it is even more important the human beings whom we wish to meet should not be lost in a welter of facts concerning taxation, land and property dues, the legal system, and the machinery of government. I was reflecting on how best to deal with these subjects when I happened to come across a picture of a boat. It shows one of the beautiful ships of which numerous models exist in the Egyptian Museum at Cairo, in the British Museum and other collections; it is reproduced opposite p. 32.

For the Egyptian the boat was his principal means of transport, and as the Nile played such an important part in his life he had every reason to expect that much of his travelling in the after-life would also be by water. So he buried these model boats in his tomb. Such boats have always fascinated me. If you look carefully you will see what a delightful craft this was, with the curving hull, the benches for the rowers, the mast and big square sail, and amidships a cabin for the owner, roofed against the fierce Egyptian sunlight, but open at the sides to admit the breeze. It was in vessels such as these that the Pharaoh, and his ministers and high officials made their journeys along the Nile, and sometimes along the Syrian coast to visit their colonies. In some of the cabins you will see a tiny effigy of the owner; even his cabin trunk is included, stowed away under his bunk.

This boat gave me an idea. It was part of the duties of high officials of Pharaoh to make periodical tours of the provinces on behalf of their royal master to visit local Governors, or "Nomarchs" (the provinces were called "Nomes") to investigate matters concerning taxation—and particularly to check extortion—to study the state of the land and the irrigation canals, to inspect garrisons, or to settle legal disputes—his functions varying according to the position he held. Let us imagine that we are travelling through Egypt in the boat of one of these high officials. The period is that of the Eighteenth Dynasty (1580-1321 B.C.) in the reign of Tuthmosis III. We are travelling in the boat of the Vizier Rekhmire. This man actually existed. His tomb is one of the most interesting to be seen in Thebes, and although this journey is imaginary it is one which he could very easily have made; and the duties he performed, which will be described as the journey proceeds, are set out in detail on the walls of his tomb.

Before we start, a word about the functions of the Vizier. He was the chief officer of state under the Pharaoh. He carried into effect all the administrative side of the royal functions, apart from the religious aspect (for the Pharaoh was also the Chief Priest). He appointed the four "reporters" who were responsible, three times a year, for a statement on the affairs of the provinces. He received the reports of the district inspectors; he attended to provincial boundaries, allocations of land, orders for second crops, inundation, tax arrears, robberies in the provinces, and the complaints of local governors.

Under him were many other officials whose high-sounding titles are inscribed in their tombs; "The Fan-bearer at the King's right hand"; "The Eyes and Ears of

the King", who made confidential inquiries; "The Messenger in the Country, who filled the heart of the King";
the tutor, "making excellent of the King"; the "Scribe of
Horus the strong bull" (i.e. the King); the "Chief of the
Guard", and many others. It is likely that some of these
officials might be travelling with the Vizier. We may
imagine, then, a small flotilla of boats moving up the
river from the Delta to Thebes, the imperial capital.

The Vizier and his staff have been on a visit to some of the
Syrian coast-towns which owe allegiance to Pharaoh, for
at this time, thanks to the conquests of Tuthmosis III,
the Egyptians control a large part of what is now Syria,
Israel and the Lebanon. Running southward before the
wind, with the mountainous Mediterranean coast away to
our left, we come at last to the coast of Egypt. Long before
we see the shore the blue sea is stained with brown mud,
which becomes denser as we approach the mouth of the
great river. Then we see the long, flat coastline, the palm
trees and the acacias, and the wide, green expanse of the
Nile Delta.

Shortly after our boat enters one of the two main branches
of the Nile the wind drops. The rowers curse under their
breath, for this means that they will have to unship their
oars and begin the long, hard pull upstream. But the
Vizier is a great man, and an impatient one. He has much
to see and do before he can arrive at his home in Thebes.
So there is nothing for it but to start rowing. Down comes
the big square sail. It is furled along the yard. The brown-
skinned sailors, naked to the waist, bend their backs, the
oars creak in steady rhythm, and from a platform near the
stern the gong sends out its brazen voice, keeping time for
the rowers. One of the men raises his voice in a monotonous chant, and with each pull at their oars the sailors
sing a refrain. The brown water rushes past the long,
curving hull and high up in the stern the steersman manipu-
lates the huge steering paddles, watching out for sandbanks,

and occasionally shouting out a greeting, or an insult, to the steersmen of passing craft.

Under an awning amidships sits the Vizier, dictating to his scribes. He wears a long white robe of gauffered linen, and the heavy black wig frames a face of great dignity. His scribes, who sit before him cross-legged, their rolls of papyrus on their knees, are more simply dressed in short white kilts. Ahead, on the poop, stands the captain, giving orders to the crew, and behind the Vizier's ship follow the other boats of the flotilla, their flashing oar-blades catching the gleam of the sun.

Only the Vizier and his high officials wear wigs. The crew is shaven-headed, and all of them wear the simple white kilt, leaving the breast bare. Fifteen hundred years ago, in the time of the Old Kingdom, when the Pyramids were built, even noblemen wore the kilt, but in these days men of rank have taken to the long robe. But there is one thing which all have in common. They are all clean-shaven. That is why it is easy to distinguish an Asiatic ship when it passes. Here comes one now, moving rapidly downstream, its cargo piled high on the deck. Even if they had not noticed its foreign rig, our crew would have known that the ship was not Egyptian, for its crew are bearded. Our men look curiously at it and the foreigners look back at us. As the two vessels pass abreast our captain sings out a greeting in a language which is not Egyptian and the foreign captain replies in the same tongue. The strangers are Syrians.

In the time of the Old Kingdom the Egyptians knew little of the world outside their own valley, but now, in the New Kingdom, they have moved out to conquer an Empire; Tuthmosis III, the greatest of the warrior Pharaohs, has led his armies as far as the Euphrates in the north-east, and has subdued the Nubians in the south. Foreign captives have been brought back to Thebes, and foreign princes are being brought up at the Pharaoh's court, and some Egyptian noblemen have married foreign wives. Nor have these contacts been achieved entirely by conquest. The Pharaoh has diplomatic and commercial relations with other powers, with the Hittite Empire, with the Kings of Babylon, and the rulers of the great maritime empire of Crete. Rekhmire knows these people well, and in his tomb, which is already in preparation in the Theban necropolis, his artists have depicted him receiving gifts from the "Sea-people" as the islanders were known to the Egyptians. Even now, as we round a bend in the river, another foreign ship comes into view, and one of Rekhmire's staff draws his attention to it. "The *Keftiu*," he says. (See illustration opposite p. 177.)

As the two ships pass the Vizier makes a courteous bow towards the Cretan official who sits under his awning, a slim-waisted man wearing a short, richly-decorated skirt, and with jewelled bracelets on his arms. The Cretan mariners, though clean-shaven, are of a different build from the Egyptians; tall and slim, with dark curling hair and long side-locks falling over one shoulder. So the vessels pass, ours going south to Thebes, the other north, to pass out into the "Great Green Sea", as the Egyptians call it, to that lonely island far out in the ocean which few Egyptians have ever seen.

We pass Buto, which was the old northern capital in ancient times, before Upper and Lower Egypt were united by Menes, the founder of the First Dynasty. Now it is just another provincial town with its temples, houses and gardens, but its ancient greatness is commemorated in one of the royal insignia which the King wears on his crown—the serpent, which was the emblem of Buto. The other royal insignia which appears beside the serpent is the falcon, the emblem of Nekhen, the old capital of southern Egypt. Although nearly 1,500 years separate Menes from the present King, Tuthmosis III, he still wears these two emblems to commemorate the unification of the two kingdoms, and one of his ceremonial titles is "King of Upper and Lower Egypt".

It will take us eight or nine days to reach Thebes, a long, wearisome journey. The Vizier prefers to work in the early morning and in the cool of the evening, reserving the afternoon for sleep. From time to time he dines in his cabin, sometimes takes a stroll on the deck and talks to the captain, and at the end of each day the boat moors at the quayside of some provincial town and Rekhmire and his staff sleep at the house of some local official.

Now it is early morning and we are leaving the Delta behind. The broad green plain begins to narrow, and to right and left the brown desert hills approach. From now on, for 300 miles, we shall never lose sight of those twin deserts, the Libyan on the west and the Arabian on the east. Far away to the right, standing on the high brown plateau are the Pyramids, golden against the morning blue of the sky. First, Dedefre's Pyramid at Abu Roash and then the familiar trio which we know as the Giza Group—the Great Pyramid of Cheops, the Pyramid of Chephren, and the small pyramid of Mycerinus. The time of which we are writing, that of Tuthmosis III, was 3,000 years and more before our epoch, yet to Rekhmire, gazing out at them from his boat, they are already ancient monuments; Cheops died more than 1,500 years before Rekhmire was born, and Cheops's Pyramid was far from being the oldest.

As we travel further south other pyramids appear out of the haze: Zawiyet-el-Arayan, Abusir (though they were not then known by these Arabic names, of course) and Sakkara. At Sakkara the great Step Pyramid rises proudly above its white enclosing wall, the work of Imhotep, architect of King Djoser, who reigned before Cheops, as did Snofru, whose pyramids greet the Vizier's gaze a few miles south of Sakkara. To Rekhmire and the men of his time these ancient Pharaohs of the Old Kingdom are almost creatures of legend. As a royal official, Rekhmire knows his history.

He knows that, in the intervening millennium dynasties have risen and fallen, and that the capital of Egypt has shifted several times. The Old Kingdom monarchs ruled from Memphis, whose towers and temples the Vizier can see rising ahead of him, opposite Djoser's Step Pyramid. Then, after some 500 years, at the end of the Sixth Dynasty, the power of the kings declined and there followed 100 years of confusion, during which the central power broke up and Egypt suffered foreign invasion. Then a new Dynasty arose, the Eleventh; new, strong kings ruled the country from Hermonthis and later from Thebes. Again, after 400 years, came collapse and the invasion of the Asiatic "Shepherd Kings". Finally, salvation had come through the warrior-kings of the Seventeenth Dynasty, who, a few hundred years before the Vizier's time, had driven out the invaders and established a stable kingdom. It was one of the successors of these kings, Tuthmosis, also a warrior, who now ruled Egypt; and Thebes, from a small provincial centre, the head of a *nome*, had become the rich and powerful capital of an Empire which stretched from the Sudan to the Euphrates.

Yes, the Vizier reflects as he disembarks at Memphis, Egypt has seen many changes since the Great Ones were buried in the pyramids which he can see on the far side of the river. Kings did not build pyramids nowadays; instead, they hollowed out deep, rock-cut tombs out of the Theban hills. Nobles like himself no longer built stone *mastabas* beside their royal master's monument. They too had their rock-cut tombs in the Necropolis, not in the Royal Valley, of course, but on the other side of the mountain. Which reminded him: he must see how his own tomb was progressing, since, like all Egyptians of rank, he was preparing his own "eternal habitation" during his lifetime.

And yet, in other ways, the Vizier knows that much remains the same, that he has inherited a tradition handed down to him from those ancient kings, the founders of the

Egyptian State. He worships the same gods as they did, using the same or similar rituals; the scenes which his artist's were even now painting on the walls of his tomb: Rekhmire receiving his food-offerings, Rekhmire supervising his farms and estates, Rekhmire entertaining his guests at a banquet, Rekhmire spearing fish in the Nile—all these can be seen in the tombs of his predecessors who had served Cheops in this town of Memphis fifteen centuries ago.

Above all, the system of law and government which it was his duty to administer had been handed down, with some modifications, from those far-off rulers.

What was this tradition of government?

First, a strong centralised power, authoritarian and absolute. The achievements of Egypt during the Old, Middle and New Kingdoms was due to the fact that the Pharaohs of that time had complete mastery of the country. Through their unchallenged control of man-power they were able to carry out public works and to raise monuments which still inspire awe even in the twentieth century.

Secondly, it was a tradition of rigid bureaucratic control. Ultimate power rested with the Pharaoh, who appointed his own ministers and officials, who were often members of the royal family. These officials held their posts by appointment or inheritance. They were rarely elected. Under them were armies of minor officials, inspectors, tax-collectors, scribes and the like. It is doubtful if any country in the world has been more highly administered than Ancient Egypt. While on the one hand this had the bad effect of tying the country in a bureaucratic net and stultifying progress, it was to some extent inevitable. The reason was that, apart from the gold mines and the spoils of foreign conquests, the wealth of Egypt lay in its manpower and its land, and the land in turn depended on the annual flooding of the Nile. It was the duty of the officials to see that this man-power was organised and effectively used, that the flooding of the river was as far as possible predicted and regulated by means of canals and irrigation works, and that the resultant wealth was channelled by taxation towards the central power.

*   *   *

Memphis, one of the cities which Rekhmire is visiting on his way south, was in ancient times the capital, but now it is simply the chief city of the Memphite *nome* or province. At this time, the period of the New Kingdom, there are sixty-seven of these *nomes*, forty-two in Upper (i.e. southern) Egypt and twenty-five in Lower Egypt. The Vizier stays the night with the Governor, and the following day consults with him on matters needing his attention. They sit, with their staff, in a columned and frescoed hall, open on one side to a garden in which fountains rustle gently above ornamental pools, and birds flit among the acacias. Local officials come and go, prostrating themselves as they enter the presence. Scribes are in attendance, sitting cross-legged on the floor and entering the Vizier's decisions on their scrolls. First there is a heated dispute about the provincial boundaries, calling for a consultation of the ancient records. Next, the delicate question of tax arrears; but then last year's crops were poor, says the Governor; a little time is needed. But the Vizier is not satisfied. Is the Governor sure that the taxes were not paid? Have not been diverted into the pockets of some local official? He has met such cases of peculation before. The Governor promises to investigate.

Next the assessment for the coming year is discussed. Experts are called in to give their opinion on the next inundation. Will it be a "good Nile" or a "bad Nile"? On the judgement of the men who study the "nilometers" which register the rise of the water, will depend the estimate of the agricultural yield and the resulting tax assessment. Then there are other questions; an adequate labour force to repair dykes and canals and perhaps build new ones. The official responsible for the *corvée* (impressment of forced labour) is called in for consultation.

The morning wears on; the sun rises higher; the Vizier and his staff begin to smother yawns. They retire for their midday meal and a rest in the heat of the afternoon. The hall is empty; the drowsy sentries lean on their spears and there is no sound but the splash of the fountains; and the faint sound of laughter and music from the women's quarters. Down on the waterfront the brothels and the beerhouses are full, where the crew while away the time until their masters return.

In the evening there are more conferences. This time the Vizier consults his "corner men", officials appointed directly by the Pharaoh and not by the Governor of the *nome*. They are District Inspectors, four in each province, and among other things they are responsible for the census lists, not only of men, but of cattle. They give their reports, but the Vizier questions them sharply. Are they sure that the lists are accurate? For Rekhmire knows only too well the habit of the *fellahin* of driving their cattle into the uplands to escape the census.

The reports of these royal officials are useful to Rekhmire because they act as a check on the local officials, who are appointed by the Provincial Governor. For many of the officials are appointed by and owe their chief loyalty to the Governor, who is from a local family. He appoints the prefects who govern the cities, the scribes of the records who kept registers of lands and deeds, the chief judges, the chiefs of police and so on. Again, the *saru*, the chiefs of the country districts, are independent of the royal service; they judge suits concerning contracts, wills and sales; they settle the *corvée* (forced labour) and local taxation. But the District Inspectors are independent of local control and report direct to the Vizier. Thus there are two interlocking systems: the council of landowners and their chief of the province; and the Vizier and his District Inspectors

observing affairs. Rekhmire and his royal master have
constantly to watch that these local princelings do not get
too powerful and independent.

But one thing all these people have in common. They
all belong to the official, administering class; and as the
Vizier and his staff are driven down to the quay again to
re-embark for their journey, they hardly glance at the
brown-skinned labourers working in the hot sun, driving
teams of oxen, bending their backs over the furrows,
widening the irrigation canals while the foremen stand
by with whips in their hands. For them, the backbone
of Egypt, life is an almost endless round of labour, only
ending in a nameless grave on the desert fringes. They do
not look up as the procession of white-robed officials drives
by, nor do they take more than a passing glance at the
flotilla of ships as it moves upstream again, while the
Governor drives back to his lodge, thinking, "Well, that's
over"—at least until the Vizier's next visit.

*   *   *

One by one the pyramids on the western bank glide by;
Dashur, where the monuments of Snofru lean against the
empty sky; Meydûm, immense and solitary; all now
deserted, plundered more than 1,000 years ago. The
valley widens, narrows, the river turns and twists between
the enclosing cliffs and then the hills step back again
and leave space for more flat, green fields, with here and
there a mud-brick village rising above the palm trees.
And now there are no more pyramids, only deserts. Our
men chant as they haul on their oars, and often the Vizier
looks up from his work to watch a boat gliding past on its
way north. Here is one with a huge 100-foot obelisk lying
along its deck. It has come from the granite quarries of
Assuan, 500 miles to the south; the laden ship sits low in the
water.[1] Here, near the banks where the papyrus marshes

[1] Some of these boats could carry 650 tons.

grow, light skiffs dart rapidly back and forth. A nobleman
in a white kilt is doing a little wildfowling. The shouts of the
hunters come faintly across the waters; white geese rise in
clouds, and a curved throwing stick soars among them.
Two of the birds fall fluttering into the water and a boat
goes out to pick them up. Once our men raise a shout and
a member of the crew hurls a harpoon at a crocodile. But
he misses, and amid the jeers of the sailors our flotilla
moves on.

We make other calls; at Abydos the Vizier goes ashore
to make an offering in the Tomb of Osiris; further upriver
he visits a town which has been raided by nomads from the
western desert. There are accusations and counter-accusa-
tions between the prefect and the commander of the local
garrison. Rekhmire reprimands both of them, but privately
decides to recommend the appointment of another commander, and the strengthening of the garrison. So it goes
on; in one place the local officials have been evading their
income tax, in another there is a dispute on the payment of
customs, and in yet another Rekhmire meets a deputation of
pilots and steersmen, who allege non-payment of their dues.
He is very glad when, at the end of the long journey, he
sees the river traffic becoming thicker, and gardens cluster-
ing along the eastern bank, and away to the right, the
serrated crest of the Theban hills, which tell him that he is
approaching the imperial capital, his home.

To the Vizier, his staff, and some of his crew the first
sight of Thebes is like the moment when, after a long
absence, a Londoner sees London, or a Parisian approaches
Paris. It is the seat of his government, the focus of his
patriotic emotion, his workshop, his playground, his
home. Also, in the case of the Egyptian, it is something
even more important, the burial-place of his ancestors.
And this double function, a home for the living and a
resting-place for the dead, is emphasised by the fact that the
city is really two towns, divided by the river. On our right

as our ship approaches the quays is a ridge of brown hills, cracked and fissured and baked by the sun. They rise abruptly from the flat river plain, and below them, with their backs to the cliffs, is a string of magnificent stone buildings; these are the funerary temples of the kings, who are now beginning to be buried in a lonely valley on the far side of the hills. In those hills is a vast Necropolis; the cliffs, and the low ground in front of them, are honeycombed with rock-cut tombs of nobles and the richer Thebans.[1] Between the cliffs and the river are large villages of mud-brick houses, populated entirely by those whose work lies in the Necropolis. Here live the embalmers, the makers of coffins and funerary furniture, the quarrymen who hollow out the tombs, and the artists and sculptors who adorn their walls. Near the temples live the priests whose duty it is to make the regular food offerings for the spirits of the dead. All, in some way or other, serve the vast, silent population whose bodies lie hidden in their dark chambers within the hills.

But turn your eyes to the left and you see a complete contrast, the city of the living—a rich, swarming, noisy city, crowded with life. Small craft dart in and out among the hundreds of ships moored at the quaysides—ships with high, curving prows and tall masts, merchant vessels unloading grain and other produce, barges freighted with stone blocks for the temples and palaces, foreign ships from Syria and from the Aegean islands, warships, and the richly gilded craft of the Pharaoh and his nobles. A dull, confused murmur floats across the water as our flotilla approaches the quayside and the sailors stand with ropes in their hands preparing to make fast. And as we look beyond the water-front we see a huddle of mud-brick walls which are ware-houses, stores, Custom houses, shops, beerhouses, brothels, and the dwellings of the poor. Beyond them, fenced in by high walls enclosing gardens, are the houses of the nobles

---

[1] Thebes is, of course, a Greek name. In the time of which we are writing the city was called No-Amun.

and the richer officials; but these too are of mud-brick and timber, and from the outside are imposing only because of their size. The only stone building of any consequence is the great Temple of Amun-Re, King of the Gods, the pylons and obelisks of which we passed on our left as we approached the city.

And now we are alongside. The Vizier's servants and guards are waiting for him at the quayside. Men in white kilts and carrying staffs clear a way for him through the crowd, the nearest members of which touch their foreheads in the dust as he passes. He mounts his gilded chariot, and then, preceded by runners, drives through the streets to his mansion in the suburbs. Rekhmire has come home.

CHAPTER III

HOUSES AND FURNITURE

HAVING tried to give the reader an impression of Egypt as it would be seen by a high official of the Eighteenth Dynasty, I am going to make a short digression into earlier Egyptian history. It is tempting immediately to follow Rekhmire into his Theban home, and to meet his wife and children. However, that would limit us too strictly to one particular period of Egyptian history, and the subject of this chapter—houses and furniture— calls for a much wider sweep. Also, we shall be in a better position to understand Rekhmire's social and domestic background if we know something of the 2,000 years of developing civilisation which lay behind it. So for the time being let us leave the Vizier to his homecoming; we shall return to him in the next chapter.

A settled home, a permanent dwelling with its furniture and equipment, is necessary for the development of certain arts and sciences. Not all of them, of course. In poetry, philosophy, and mathematics the nomadic Arabs reached heights which the Egyptians never attained. But even the Arabs were unable to achieve their miracles of architecture and design until they established cities. The Ancient Egyptians, although they were among the first—perhaps the first—people to develop the art of writing, and produced a literature, were a long-settled people whose greatest triumphs were in architecture, sculpture and painting. Also, because they were a settled people, they early developed the art of government and civil administration.

Climate and available building materials decide the form of a people's buildings. In northern Europe with its

harsh winters and great forests, timber was the first building
material to be used when men moved down into the low-
lands from their rough stone huts on the treeless moors;
but as soon as they had learned the art of working stone
they began to build in this material or in brick; durability
and protection from wind, rain, snow and ice were and are
essential. In Egypt these conditions obviously do not
apply. The country enjoys almost perpetual sunshine, and
during many months of the year the climate is uncomfort-
ably hot, especially in the south. The main need was for
shelter from the sun and the cold night air. Stone existed in
abundance, but even after the Egyptians had settled in the
Nile Valley they rarely used stone for domestic buildings.
They used instead that which remains to this day the
cheapest, most accessible and most easily workable building
material in Egypt—*mud*.

To people living in more temperate climates mud would
seem a messy, impermanent, unsatisfactory medium. Not
so in Egypt. I have seen *mastaba* tombs at Sakkara, and
near the Great Pyramid at Giza, built of dried mud-brick
which have survived for more than 5,000 years. Earlier in
this book I have stated that the reason for the disappearance
of Ancient Egyptian towns was the perishable nature of the
building material. This, however, was due only to the fact
that it is easy to destroy, and as the Egyptians had no reason
to preserve their old homes when they wanted new ones
they simply pulled them down and built again; with their
tombs it was different, and the chief damage to these was
done by the tomb-robbers.

When the Nile recedes it leaves acres of brown mud
which rapidly turns to grey under the sun. As it dries it
splits, and in the early days of Egyptian civilisation the
people probably built their dwellings from these naturally
formed blocks, as some of the *fellahin* do to-day. But later
they learned to make blocks by mixing the mud with water.
Often the blocks were strengthened by mixing in straw and

cattle-dung. To this day the *fellahin* live in a village of mud and dung, which have a strange unfinished appearance. There is, of course, no need for a sloping roof to drain off the rain so the roofs are left flat, usually with the unfinished walls projecting irregularly above. The flat roofs are pleasant to sit on in the cool of the evening, and in Old Cairo, where ground space is restricted, many people keep their animals up there; it is quite common, when walking through the Old City, to look up and meet the reflective gaze of a cow. The reason for leaving the side-walls unfinished is to allow for the addition of another storey if necessary.

The villages and towns of Ancient Egypt were very like this, as we know from the numerous examples of model mud-brick houses, called "soul-houses" which the Ancient Egyptians left in their tombs. There are illustrations on the opposite page.

There were other building materials; timber (though at first this was sparingly used as there are no big timber-trees in Egypt), palm-ribs, reeds, and the stalks of the papyrus plant which then grew plentifully along the river-banks. Petrie, whose *Social Life in Ancient Egypt* is one of the most useful sources of information, believes that in pre-Dynastic times (before 3200 B.C.) the early chiefs had portable timber houses which, during the inundation could be moved up to the desert in a day, and in spring, when the pastures were green, could be moved down among the reed-huts of the shepherds.

"The planks, about 12 to 14 inches wide, and 6 to 7 feet high, were set upright, overlapping so as to form a panel-pattern. Being lashed together at the edges, the overlap was kept close, and slid to and fro, as the night dews or sirocco expanded or contracted the wood. The doorways were all along the sides, so as to give plenty of air when still and warm. They projected into the hall, and so left sleeping places between each, where the chief's followers could sleep as a guard around the hall. This pattern of house gave rise to the copying of external panelling *in brick work*

(our italics) for the 'eternal house' of the dead chief, a pattern
which lasted down to the Eighteenth Dynasty."

The palm ribs, or reeds, lashed together in bundles and
bound with mud, were used as pillars before these were
made of wood or stone; even to-day one can see such pillars
supporting the heavy *shaduf* or water-hoist which the
fellah uses to raise water from a lower to a higher canal.
But the most interesting point is that when, round about
2800 B.C., the Egyptians began to build monumentally in
stone, they imitated these earlier forms. Thus at Sakkara,
near the Step Pyramid of Djoser, one can see fluted columns,
which anticipate the Doric column by more than 2,000 years,
the form of which may have been derived from the bundles
of reeds which originally supported the roofs of mud-brick
houses. Another use of reeds, and palm-ribs, was to mix
them with mud and lay them across the timber rafters of a
house as roofing. This method is still in use throughout
Egypt. Logs of wood were used in pre-Dynastic times as
door-lintels, and you can still see the cylindrical form
imitated in stone above the "false doors" of the later stone
mastabas.[1]

Another feature of all except the very poorest Egyptian
houses, in ancient times and to-day, is the courtyard. In
a country such as Egypt, with its almost perpetual sunshine, the courtyard is the natural place for daily life. So
that in nearly all these model houses you will notice a walled
court in front of the house, or in the case of larger houses,
there is a courtyard with rooms opening off it on all four
sides; often there is a stone tank for water in the centre of
the court; one can see a similar arrangement in the Roman
Villas of Pompeii. There, as in Egypt, the household looked
inwards, not outwards. The Egyptian houses presented a
forbidding exterior: blank mud-brick walls pierced, high
up, by very small windows. So fierce is the Egyptian

---

[1] A rectangular tomb with sloping sides, so called because it recalls the shape of
the *mastaba*, or stone bench, outside Arab houses.

sunlight that only small apertures are necessary to illuminate
the interior. Inside the house the rooms facing the inner
courtyard often had no windows; the reflected sunlight was
sufficient to light the interior of the rooms, which were
usually open on the side facing the court. There were also
broad loggias, supported on pillars, overlooking cool,
shady gardens, all surrounded by high walls which shut
them from the outside world. It was the exact opposite of
life in northern Europe, where the windows look outward
on to the street. In Egypt they looked inward.

Gradually, over the centuries, certain features of Egyptian
houses changed; the homes of the nobles became larger and
more luxurious; pillars of stone or timber replaced those of
palm-ribs, and the mud-brick walls were coated with fine
plaster and adorned with coloured frescoes. But it is
doubtful if the houses of the very poor altered very much.

With certain exceptions there was little attempt at town-
planning. Great cities like Memphis and Thebes simply
grew haphazardly, like medieval London. Even at Akhnaten's "new" city at Tell-el-Amarna, although the main
thoroughfares are laid out in a roughly rectilinear pattern,
the suburbs straggle off in a bewildering tangle of lanes and
alleys. The only exceptions occurred when the Pharaoh
ordered some big public works and a town was specially
created to house the workmen. I have seen one such city at
Medinet Habu. It is like a barracks; straight, narrow streets
built at right angles, and hundreds of small, rectangular
houses of practically identical pattern. Petrie describes another
of these towns, at Kahun, built in the Twelfth Dynasty.

"The houses may be of any size, from four rooms to six, and
each street contains a uniform size of house. The streets vary in
length; one is 62 feet long for two houses, others are 230 feet
long for eight or nine houses. . . . The streets vary from 11 to 15
feet wide. They had a channel down the middle for a drain, like
the old English kennel. There was no separate footway, because
there were no vehicles in such a town.

"The simple houses had an open court opposite to the entrance, a common room on one side, and the store rooms on the other, with a stairway up to the roof. The larger type for artisans had an open court, four rooms opening off it, and five others dependent on the outer rooms. . . . The fire was usually against one side of a room, with a few bricks to support the cooking pots. The doors were of wood, with wooden sills and a lintel built into the wall; when the pivot holes were worn down a bit of leather was put under the pivot, usually a bit of worn-out sandal. . . ."

Allowing for the difference of climate and custom, such artisan's houses were probably superior to the "back-to-back" workers' dwellings in Britain's industrial North.

Sanitation and drainage, as we understand them, were never developed as they were by some other ancient cultures—for example, by the Minoans of Crete. At Knossos the great Palace of Minos, parts of which were built 2,000 years before Christ, had an elaborate and scientific system of drainage. Rainwater was carried from the roof through pipes let into the walls, and from thence into underground sewers big enough to accommodate a stooping man. Waste water from bathrooms was led away to these pipes, and in the Queen's Megaron there survives to this day a primitive w.c. which Sir Arthur Evans believed had a system for flushing the basin. The Ancient Egyptians did not have such an elaborate system for the simple reason that they did not need it. Roofs were drained in order to prevent water collecting and causing leaks, but, unlike Crete, Egypt has so little rainfall that underground street drainage was unnecessary.

The disposal of refuse and human excrement was another matter. In the poorer parts of the towns refuse was probably left lying about to be devoured by scavenger dogs and birds, as it still is in many Egyptian towns to-day. My reason for believing this is that in the ancient medical papyri which have come down to us, a high proportion of the cases with which the Ancient Egyptian doctors had to deal were eye diseases, which are still the scourge of Egypt. These diseases, trachoma and ophthalmia, are carried by the flies which breed among refuse. Incidentally, the other prevalent Egyptian disease, bilharzia or schistosomiasis, also occurred in Ancient Egypt. It is caused by a small worm which gets into the bloodstream and causes obstruction in the liver, heart or lungs; the disease is propagated by the *fellah's* insanitary habit of defecating and urinating in or near the canals and irrigation ditches. Tiny organisms from the stools or urine of an infected person enter into the bodies of certain species of snails, where they breed and produce other organisms which penetrate the skin and enter the bloodstream, where they develop into the bilharzia worm. Specimens of these worms have been found in Ancient Egyptian mummies.

However, before we condemn the poor Egyptian peasant for his insanitary habits, we should bear in mind his working conditions. For most of his day he worked on the land, which meant that he was always in or near water, for the fertility of the soil depended on a network of canals and ditches. Even if the *fellahin* had latrines in their homes they were only there at night. During the day he had no choice.

Earth closets have been found in the ruins of large and small Egyptian houses, though it does not seem to be known whether these were connected to an underground cesspit, or cleared daily. Personally, I suspect that the cesspit method was known. At several villages in Lower Egypt Egyptian and European doctors, who are trying to improve sanitary conditions, showed me the *fellahin's* own system of dealing with human refuse which is certainly very ancient. These villagers dig a deep pit and line it with hard-baked brick which is impervious to water, and over which the latrine is built. At the end of several months they open the pit, clean out the refuse, and after leaving it to the sun for a period in order to kill the poisons, spread it on their land as a fertiliser. This method may have been used in Pharaonic times.

The palaces of the kings and the mansions of the great were, of course, far more beautiful and luxurious than the homes of lesser men, and by the Eighteenth Dynasty, when Rekhmire lived, they had reached a pitch of comfort and refinement which could hardly be improved even at the present day; in fact, I suspect that in some respects they were probably more comfortable, and certainly far better adapted to the climate, than the blocks of European-type flats which the rich modern Egyptian inhabits on the outskirts of Cairo.

They were still built of mud-brick blocks, but the walls were adorned with delicate frescoes in gay colours, of trees and plants and birds. Some delightful examples of these were discovered by Sir Flinders Petrie at Tell-el-Amarna, and can be seen in the Ashmolean Museum at Oxford. In size and plan these houses varied according to the wealth and status of the owner, but certain basic features remained constant. First, there was a high outer wall and enclosing a garden. This wall was pierced by one sole entrance, which admitted the visitor to the porter's lodge. If it was a very large house, there would be three passages from this lodge: one to the best rooms of the house, with columned halls for reception, and smaller rooms for dining and sleeping; the second leading to the women's quarters, which were separate from those of the men; here lived the lord's harem. The third passage led to the servants' quarters, with its dining-hall, kitchens and store-rooms. The family rooms comprised about sixteen rooms, with three halls of columns; the women's quarters contained twelve rooms or more, with perhaps one hall of columns; while the kitchen and stores comprised about fourteen rooms, with a servants' hall. Right at the back of the house would be a large open court with a shady colonnade, and perhaps more store-rooms. There would thus be about fifty to sixty rooms in all, all approached by one narrow entrance for protection. This is the kind of house in which lived very high officials like Rekhmire.

There was also a somewhat smaller type of house used by the middle-class officials. These houses were about 50 feet square surrounded by a garden wall, pierced as usual by one door leading to the porter's lodge. From there you would walk along an open loggia on the north side of the house, to reach the central hall of columns. From this four groups of rooms opened, the master's room with its bed, the women's quarters and the kitchen, the men's quarters, sometimes with a secondary hall, and a group of small store-rooms. From here stairs led up to the roof. The floors of these rooms were usually paved, and if the ground was damp the Egyptians had an ingenious system of sinking short cylinders, like drain-pipes, vertically in the ground, and laying a brick paving on top of them.

It will be seen that the household of an Egyptian official of high rank was a large one. Not only were there rooms for himself, his guests and his servants, but also for his grown-up children, if they were unmarried, and for the children of his several wives. There would also be accommodation for his chariots and horses, store-rooms for food, cellars for wine, and conical granaries for grain. These were sometimes in the garden, but in small houses they were built on the roof. The picture opposite p. 34 will help to explain the layout of one of these large houses.

But it should always be remembered that most of the life of the Ancient Egyptians was lived out of doors, as it is in southern Europe to-day. The rooms were only used at night and during the winter months. It would be in the courts and gardens that we would find the Egyptian official taking his relaxation. They were great garden-lovers, perhaps out of defiance towards the grim, sterile deserts which hemmed them in. Trees were brought from Asia to supplement the few indigenous Egyptian species, carefully planted and tenderly nurtured. There were trees for fruit and trees for shade, but the bright light would penetrate the leaves, allowing for the free growth of plants and flowers underneath. Then there were big ornamental tanks for fish, which served a double purpose—for ornament and to keep down mosquitoes. Malaria does not seem to have been a serious problem in Ancient Egypt, probably for this reason.

A great gardener could rise to high rank. One of the most charming tombs in the Theban Necropolis is that of Senufer, Head Gardener to the King. The rough rock ceiling is left in its natural state, and painted to represent vine trellises, so that one appears to be walking under clusters of hanging grapes. Only a man of importance would be allowed to make a tomb in the Necropolis, or indeed could afford one.

The furniture of Egyptian homes varied with the importance of the owner, but, generally speaking, there was less of it than in European or American houses. However, in the homes of the kings and the nobles such furniture as did exist was beautiful to look at and finely made. The principal articles were beds, chairs, tables, and chests for clothes and other articles. Lovely examples of these have been preserved in Egyptian tombs, mainly of the Eighteenth and Nineteenth Dynasties, and other examples are depicted on the wall-reliefs and paintings.

To take the chairs first; there would be fewer of these than in a European house of comparable size, because the Egyptians had the Oriental habit of sitting or half-kneeling on the floor or on cushioned divans. Guests at parties are often shown in this posture, with their knees tucked under them (see illustration facing p. 48). They never seem to have adopted a reclining position when dining, as did the Greeks and Romans.

Nor did they sit around a communal dining table. The tables depicted in tomb-paintings were small affairs and at a party each guest would have his own table, set with delicacies which were served to him by a slave.

Describing the construction of this furniture, Petrie writes:

"The design of Egyptian furniture is always excellent, mechanically. The joints have angle pieces of naturally-bent grain. The chair backs are well supported with diagonal struts behind, like old Windsor chairs. The tall thin legs of tables are held in by a crossbar and diagonal struts. The lines of couches and chairs are flowing and harmonious, the proportions look safe and true, without being clumsy. A most ingenious form of spring served for suspending the portable shrines; straight at one end and curved at the other, the weight, which was hung near each end, contracted the straight length and expanded the curve, so that the total length, framed in, remained equal."

Personally, I find some Eighteenth Dynasty furniture over-ornate. The famous Throne of Tutankhamun is to my mind clumsy and overloaded with ornament. I prefer the charming child's chair (opposite p. 35) of wood inlaid with ivory, which was also found in the tomb and was presumably used by the King when he was a small boy. Even more vulgar were some of the palace ornaments found in Tutankhamun's tomb. Take the well-known boat-shaped shrine of alabaster. It is beautifully made, and the material is lovely, but, apart from the charming little figure of Queen Ankhesnamun with her fan (she sits in the prow of the boat), the article seems to me not much better than certain specimens of Victoriana.

Hardly any furniture has come down to us from the Old Kingdom, but the few examples which have survived, with representations on wall-reliefs, indicate that the standard of design was far higher in the time of the Pyramid-builders. Some of the simplicity, strength and majesty which one sees in the diorite statue of Chephren seems to have entered into the design of such furniture. The most superb example is, of course, the bed, chair, canopy and carrying-chair of

Queen Hetephras, the mother of Cheops, which was found, with her empty sarcophagus, in a deep shaft near the Great Pyramid.

Ancient Egyptian beds are interesting. They are built much higher off the ground than the beds of to-day, and sometimes the mattress sloped slightly from head to foot. The bed-frames were formed from massive poles tapering at the ends. The mitre-jointing was very varied, six different types of join have been identified. The mattress itself was of cord matting, stretched tightly, but having a certain resilience. They were presumably covered with cushions, and people who have slept on them say they are quite comfortable. Petrie even alleged that the wooden head-rest was comfortable, but this I find hard to believe. These semi-circular head-rests have always been something of a puzzle to modern minds. They are still in use to-day in certain parts of Africa, and were shaped to fit under the neck, near the ears, presumably in order to keep the heavy wigs which the Egyptians wore clear of the bed. But it is difficult to see why they did not take their wigs off at night. Perhaps they only used these rests when relaxing during the day. Petrie also alleged, on what grounds I cannot discover, that the Ancient Egyptians slept in a "straight-out" position, whereas most of us to-day curl up. He points out that the bodies of the pre-Dynastic Egyptians were buried in a crouching position, knees under the chin, whereas during Dynastic times they were buried, lying straight; but burial customs are no indication of sleeping habits.

It must not be thought that all Egyptian furniture was well-made. The Egyptians were as familiar as we are with the jerry-builder and the maker of gimcrack furniture. Sometimes he would fake a mortice-and-tenon joint, allowing the tenon to penetrate only a short distance into the wood and then clapping on a piece of inlay on the other side to make it appear that the joint went right through. Cheap wood was covered with veneer; ivory inlays were imitated with white paint. As for "graining" with paint, there was no trick used by the Victorian faker which the Egyptians did not know. They imitated grained-wood patterning, with all the characteristic knots and undulations, as far back as the Third Dynasty (2800 B.C.); they even imitated valuable stone vases in wood. Granite was faithfully copied in paint, and at Amarna limestone columns were found painted to represent glazed tiles; even inlaid jewellery was imitated with coloured glazes.

If the Egyptians of the New Kingdom had shared our passion for antiquity, no doubt they would have produced "genuine antiques" of the Old Kingdom to sell to collectors. Fortunately for archaeologists they did not, which is just as well; the skilful fakes of their modern descendants are quite difficult enough to deal with.

Other articles of furniture in Egyptian homes were chests for linen, clothes, arms and other articles. These were often beautifully made and inlaid with ivory, lapis-lazuli, carnelian and other materials. The finest examples are those found in the tomb of Tutankhamun. Lighting was by oil lamps, and some of these were of thin translucent alabaster, painted with a coloured design on the inside which showed through when a wick was lit inside the lamp. There were also miniature shrines containing figures of Amun, Isis, Osiris and other gods. In the houses of the King and his wealthier subjects gold and silver were frequently used in furniture and ornaments. An Egyptian feast, with the soft light gleaming on the gold and silver of the furniture, bringing out the glow of red carnelian and green lapis-lazuli, must have been a beautiful sight, especially when one adds to it the glitter of bracelets and necklaces and the jewels of the women.

But what did they eat? Among the wealthier classes the diet seems to have been rich and varied. In tomb-paintings of feasts we see fowl, probably boiled, grilled or roasted; and beef was also eaten, either roasted or grilled. In their prayers for the deceased the Egyptians asked that his nourishment in Heaven should be bread and beer, beef and goose. Ten different sorts of meat are mentioned, five kinds of birds, and eleven varieties of fruit, "and all manner of sweet things". Fashion entered a lot into eating, the favourite dishes varying from age to age—again among the rich. Erman points out in his *Life in Ancient Egypt* that a Nineteenth Dynasty King had set down in an inscription the meals he ate on a journey through various towns with his court, and "in the list of ten varieties of bread and five sorts of cake there is scarcely one which was in common use under the Old Empire."

Like us, they occasionally liked to try foreign dishes, and in one sacred book it is stated that the gods "eat the fine bread of *Quamh*"—a Semitic speciality.

They obtained good wine from Charu, beer from Quede, fine oil from "Ersa, Cheta, Sangar and T'echesa"—all foreign towns.

As to the preparation of food, not much is known. Goose, the favourite national dish, was roasted over live embers. Fish was roasted in the same way.

Bread-making was always very important. Probably the Egyptians had no mills. They pounded the corn with great pestles. Finer flour was obtained by rubbing the corn between two stones. Then they kneaded the dough (usually the women performed this task and there are many models showing the process) and then the round flat cakes were lightly baked over the coals. Some of the shapes in which the cakes were made are remarkably like modern pastries. But I suspect that they tasted very like Arab bread to-day—like tough cardboard.

Beer and wine were the staple drinks. Beer was the favourite drink of the Egyptian people and there are many models from Twelfth Dynasty towns showing the brewing process. Beer was made from ground barley, or, as it was called, "the corn of Upper Egypt". Under the Old Empire there were four kinds, including "black beer" and "beer of a dark colour."

Wine was drunk by the kings and nobles, and in the Palace of Akhnaten, excavated at Tell-el-Amarna by Petrie and others, wine jars have been found inscribed with the vintage. Judging from some of the poems and tomb-inscriptions drunkenness was common, in fact encouraged. But although the results of excess are vividly depicted, there is no record of a hang-over cure!

When eating the Ancient Egyptians of the Old Kingdom squatted on the ground, though in Rekhmire's time chairs and stools were used by people of importance. They ate with their hands, and after eating, water was poured over the hands, as in the Orient to-day. One sees depicted in the dining-rooms of the great, jugs and basins almost exactly like a Victorian wash-stand. The tables were decked with flowers, and the guests wore flowers in their hair. The love of flowers and green plants was always a characteristic of the Ancient Egyptian people.

And now, having learned something of their houses, their furniture and domestic habits, let us meet the people themselves.

CHAPTER IV

THE VIZIER GIVES A PARTY

H AVING rested after his long journey and made his report to Pharaoh, Rekhmire has now decided to celebrate his homecoming with a party, to which we are invited.

Across the river, the sun is setting behind the Theban hills, and in the great temple of Amun-Re the priests are chanting their last offices, their hands outstretched to Re as he goes to "his Horizon". After the stupefying heat of the day, a refreshing coolness begins to descend upon Thebes, reviving and stimulating the city. Down by the quaysides the boatmen shout to each other; music and hand-clapping float out from the beer-shops and eating-houses along the water-front; a woman leans out of an upper window and calls to a passing sailor, whose rude reply provokes a stream of answering abuse.

Petitioners who have waited vainly all afternoon at the gateway of some great official get wearily to their feet, wrap their cloaks around them and pad their way home along the narrow streets, their bare feet kicking up little puffs of grey dust.

We will assume we are Theban residents living a little distance from the Vizier's house. At the appointed time the chariot is brought round by our servants. We mount, and, accompanied by two or three runners with torches, begin our brief drive. The streets are crowded. Often we have to pull to the side of the narrow road to allow a string of cattle to pass; once, at a cross-roads, we are held up for five minutes while a detachment of soldiers marches past, the bare-chested men carrying spears and shields, their officers marching ahead of them. Then the streets begin to widen; we drive past high walls over which palm trees peep, and the porters sit outside their lodges on three-legged stools, enjoying the evening air and chatting with their friends. Once a dog rushes out of an alleyway, snapping at our horses' heels until driven off by the driver. The air is warm and soft, so that we need only our lightest clothes, though the servants have brought wraps for the return journey.

Now we have arrived. Our chariot draws up beside the great wall of the Vizier's house. The porter, in his best clothes and carrying his staff of office, stands by the lighted doorway directing the servants. Some come forward to direct our driver where to put the chariot. As we alight and mount the steps other chariots are arriving with guests, slim men and elegant women in spotless robes of gauffered linen, and wearing heavy black curled wigs which frame their faces. There is much laughter and conversation as friends greet each other. And now, preceded and followed by male and female slaves, we are passing along the long corridor beside the house which leads to the main reception-room, the hall of columns.

As we enter we are met by more slaves and handmaidens, the men wearing the short white kilt, starched and projecting in front, the girls wearing practically nothing except wisps of fabric round the loins, and necklaces, bracelets and anklets of coloured beads. They flit in and out among the white-robed guests, presenting to each a lotus-flower, and handing round small dainties and cups of wine or beer. This, of course, is before the main meal, which will be served when the visitors are seated.

Now we are in the lofty hall of columns, which are painted a dark red, with capitals shaped like a lotus-bud. The soft light from the alabaster lamps shines on the coloured frescoes which adorn the walls—trees with birds of plumage flitting among the branches, flowers and butterflies delicately drawn on the smooth plaster. The eye travels up the columns, past the coloured capitals, to the rafters of the ceiling, which are also gaily patterned. There is a babel of conversation as we edge our way through the throng of bare-shouldered women and dark, heavily-wigged men to the place where the Vizier waits to greet us at the far end of the hall.

Rekhmire is a noble figure in his stiffly-starched robe of fine linen, pleated in many folds, and held in by a richly-ornamented girdle. His shrewd, humorous eyes smile at us from under the black wig, and as he stretches out his hand to greet you the gold bracelets gleam on his arms. Beside him stands the lady Meryet, his Chief Wife, who, like all Egyptian women of rank, shares many of her husband's activities. She also is of noble birth, and, as Tiyi—the uncharitable wife of the Chief Secretary—will tell you, Rekhmire did very well by marrying her, as her fortune was larger than his. The high status which Egyptian women enjoy is due in part to the fact that inheritance is always through the female line. Even the Pharaoh himself could only be King by marrying the royal heiress.

Meryet is a handsome woman. She is about thirty-five, twenty years younger than her husband, and though she is no longer as slim as her daughters, her figure is still good, set off by the clinging robe of almost transparent linen which frankly reveals its outlines. She too wears the large wig of natural hair, curled in hundreds of tight plaits, which hangs almost to her bare shoulders. There are gold bracelets on her rounded arms, her finger- and toe-nails are dyed with henna, and her dark eyes are made to appear even larger and more elongated by the green-blue eye-paint which she has applied to them. She has spent the better part of the afternoon on her toilette and is a credit to her handmaidens.

Near her stand the two loveliest of her daughters, similarly dressed. The eldest is Nofret, tall, slim, and rather imperious (she is a priestess of Amun, entitled to

shake the *systrum* before Pharaoh as he enters the Temple to
offer sacrifice), but rather a trial to her mother and the
despair of several young men who had hopes of marrying
her. Her younger sister, Ta-kha'et, though she has not the
cold, classical beauty of Nofret, makes up for it by her
animation and intelligence. She is seventeen, a little shorter
than her sister, and is enjoying herself. Part of her joy
arises from the fact that, unlike many of her father's parties,
this one, at her request, is not only for the elderly Court
officials, but for their sons and daughters. Not that the
daughters interest Ta-kha'et very much. She has met them
all before, often. But she rarely has the opportunity of
meeting the young men, in one of whom, Sinuhe, the son of
the Chief Secretary, she has more than a passing interest.
Tiyi—Sinuhe's mother—thinks Ta-kha'et is a minx. So
does Sinuhe, but in a different way.

Here is Tiyi approaching now, a thin, tight-lipped
woman with the darting eyes of a bird. Meryet greets her
with insincere but well-simulated cordiality; Tiyi has
always been one of her trials. She knew, of course, that
Rekhmire had to invite the Chief Secretary, who is one of
the highest officials at court, but oh, his wife. . . . Tiyi
passes on into the crowd to take her seat, and Meryet, after
remarking quietly to her husband, "Where on *earth* did she
get those ear-rings?" reassumed her smile for the next guest.

Standing beside the Vizier himself is his youngest adult
son, a handsome, eighteen-year-old lad named Kenamun.
Rekhmire's eldest sons, Menkheperre-Sonb and Amenhotep,
are married. They and their wives are among the guests.
Kenamun is an officer in the troop of picked soldiers who
form the Palace Guard, known as the "Followers of His
Majesty"—a post he obtained through his father's influence.
But he is a restless, ambitious young man, already tiring of
ceremonial duties and anxious for a little action. As he
dutifully smiles and greets his father's guests his eyes are
searching the crowd for the one man he wishes to see, and

whom Rekhmire has said will be present. This is General
Amenemhab, hero of several foreign campaigns and much
admired by the young soldier. Kenamun is secretly hoping
that, if the General likes him, he might persuade his father
—and, even more important, his mother—to let him be
transferred to foreign service. Ah, there is the General
coming in now, a man of forty-five, with powerful, sun-
tanned face and an erect, muscular figure. He smiles at
Rekhmire across the room and Kenamun gives his father a
curious, hopeful glance.

Other notable guests come forward, make their greetings,
and move on to the room where the banquet has been
prepared; the Mayor of Thebes and his wife and son; the
Fanbearer to the King[1] and his wife; the Chief Priest of
Amun and his wife and daughter; the Keeper of the Royal
Garden and his fat, homely spouse; the Royal Tutor; and
the Chief Scribe and his melancholy-looking son, who is an
officer of chariotry. His name is Senmut; he is a high-born
but rather shy youth believed to be in love with Nofret.

So, gradually, they move out of the Hall of Reception
to another columned room, where gold and inlaid chairs
are arranged, in order of precedence, for the more distinguished guests. The others seat themselves on the straw
mats and cushions spread around the floor, the women
gracefully arranging their narrow skirts and adjusting their
curled wigs. (For the manner of sitting, see the illustration
of a banquet opposite p. 48.) The girl slaves hang garlands
of flowers round the necks of the guests, and hand to each
a cake of scented grease which he or she places on top of his
or her wig. During the course of the evening this will
gradually melt and anoint the face and neck, which apparently gives great pleasure.

Now the feast begins. Around the room are set many
small tables on which the food is set; roast beef, chicken,

[1] The bearer of this strange-sounding title was one of the most important officers
in the realm, a kind of Grand Chamberlain. The office sounds servile, but compare
the modern "Gentleman of the Bedchamber" and the "Mistress of the Robes".

duck, pigeon, vegetables, and a large variety of bread cut into different shapes. Nearby stand the wine jars set in metal stands, each jar marked with the vintage year. Rekhmire is noted for his fine cellar, and as the bronze wine-cups are rapidly filled and re-filled the conversation becomes more animated. Meanwhile, the slaves, male and female, serve the guests with delicacies, which are eaten with the hand, knives only being used to cut the meat. Little Nebet, the eight-year-old daughter of Meryet, who sits beside her mother's chair, is manfully tackling a small chicken, while her elder brother Per-hor, aged ten, is gnawing a grilled chop. Napkins and finger-bowls are handed round so that the guests can deal with the grease on their hands; the steward of the household energetically directs the servants.[1]

The guests are beginning to split up into conversational groups. Rekhmire is talking to General Amenemhab about his recent trip. Young Kenamun sits beside his father, listening to every word.

"I talked to Merire at Asiut," says the Vizier. "They've had trouble with the Libyans again; the third raid in twelve months."

"I heard about it, of course," replies the General.

"They caught the garrison napping. Fifty men killed in their beds before they could reach their arms. By the time the alarm was given the raiders were away, with half the women and most of the stores."

Amenemhat frowns and looks at his ring. "I know," he

[1] Although social life was much freer among the Ancient Egyptians than it is among the Arabs, unmarried men and women were not allowed to mix as freely as they do in the west to-day. In noble houses the women lived in their own quarters, but on occasions like this both sexes could be present, as we know from many tomb-paintings of the period. At the same time it seems probable that only the married couples sat together; unchaperoned meetings between young people of opposite sexes would be frowned upon, as they are in Oriental and some Western countries to this day. Nevertheless, from what we know of human nature, it is not unlikely that these barriers were occasionally crossed; for the purpose of this episode I am going to assume that they were.

I am also well aware that Oriental marriages are usually "arranged" on a basis of family alliances and property, but if I am asked to believe that young people in Ancient Egypt never fell in love, I can only express my polite disbelief.

said. "Merire sent me a full report, and I've had another from the garrison commander."

"Pewero?" The Vizier raises his eyebrows. "What do you think of him?"

"Not much."

"Neither does the Governor."

"I'd have had him transferred months ago, but the man I had in mind as a replacement was away in Nubia. Anyway, you'll be pleased to hear that Pewero's being recalled. The new man will leave to-morrow."

"Good."

A little distance away Meryet is talking to the wife of the Royal Tutor, who is fingering her hostess's necklace.

"It's lovely, dear," says the Tutor's wife. "Syrian?"

"Yes; my husband brought it back from Gebal—and this," she adds, holding out her arm on which a bracelet glitters. "Those are from Gebal too," she says, nodding towards a group of fine vases which stand on a nearby table. "Oh, and some wonderful Tyrian dyed cloth—bales of it!"

"I wish my husband could travel," sighs the Tutor's wife.

"Oh, I don't know," replies Meryet, taking another slice of chicken. "Rekhmire's always away for so long; one misses him—and then the boys tend to get out of hand when their father's away."

"Per-hor looks very well, anyway," remarks her friend, nodding towards Meryet's small son, who is showing the General a model soldier which Rekhmire has brought back from his travels. His small sister, Nebet, not to be outdone, runs forward dragging a toy horse on wheels (see illustration opposite p. 96). Meryet gently pulls the child towards her, wipes Nebet's greasy little mouth, and beckons to a stout woman slave. "They're getting unruly," she says. "Take Nebet to bed and tell Per-hor that he must go too."

Reluctantly the two children allow themselves to be

dragged away by the stout nurse, one on each arm; the guests wave to them as they leave the room.

Meryet holds out her cup to be refilled, and resumes the interrupted conversation.

"It's not Per-hor who worries me," she says. "I can cope with him. It's Kenamun. He thinks of nothing but the Army. I thought he would be satisfied when my husband got him into the Royal Bodyguard, but he's not. He wants to go campaigning, like Senmut over there. You see? Kenamun's got him in a corner; talking about the Syrian campaign, I'll be bound."

For Kenamun, tiring over the conversation between his father and the General, has found his way to the melancholy young man, Senmut, an officer of charioteers, who has served in Pharaoh's Syrian campaigns. Senmut, who is watching Nofret on the far side of the room, has only half an ear for Kenamun's eager questions.

"But how high are the mountains?"

"Enormous."

"Higher than the Theban hills?"

Senmut laughs. "You could put twenty of the Theban hills on top of each other and still they'd be lower than the Syrian mountains. And they're cold—by Horus, they're cold." Senmut shivered in recollection. "That's why the Syrians wear such heavy clothes." He smiled again, "Perhaps that's why they wear beards—to keep their faces warm."

Kenamun laughs too, but he is puzzled. Like most Egyptians, he has never seen a mountain, never known any climate but the warm, flat valley of the Nile.

"And there is a Nile in the sky?" he inquires.

"That's what the priests say. The water comes from the sky, it's true, but it isn't a river. It's rain."

"But we have rain here sometimes," objects Kenamun.

"You call *that* rain," laughs his companion. "Here you get only a sprinkle, which dries in an hour. There you get storms, torrents which last for days and weeks. And snow."

"Snow? What's that?"

"We haven't even a word for it in our language. It's white. It falls from the sky like rain—and it's terribly cold. Your bones ache; all feeling goes from your hands. You can't fasten your harness and you can't feel your bow-string. Seth himself invented snow."

"Still, I would like to go," sighs Kenamun. Then he looks curiously at Senmut, who has taken a thin roll of papyrus out of his robe.

"What's that?" asks the Vizier's son.

Senmut, who still has his eyes on Nofret, who is surrounded by a group of young girls, replies:

"I'll tell you later. Oh good, the dancers are coming. Is Mutardis still in the house?"

"Oh yes," replies the young man. "My father still dotes on her. I think she's getting a bit fat."

"Shhh!" warns Senmut as from the far end of the columned hall a group of singers and musicians enters.

"It's all right," says Kenamun. "These are only the men. *She* comes on later."

The musicians come on to the centre of the floor; they are all men, wearing the familiar white kilt, with ornaments on their breasts and arms. Some carry instruments—a harp, lyres, several flutes, and small square drums. The instrumentalists seat themselves on the floor. The flutes begin to wail, the harp and lyres pluck out the accompaniment, while the palms of the drummers keep up a rhythmic patter.

They sing songs in honour of the god Amun-Re. No doubt Rekhmire, knowing that the High Priest of Amun would be present, has arranged this:

"How happy is the temple of Amun, even she that spendeth her days in festivity with the King of the Gods within her.

"She is like a woman drunken, who sitteth outside the chamber, with loosened hair. . . ."

At this point Meryet interrupts her conversation with the Mayor's wife to remark:

"Look. Nozme's getting drunk again."

It is true. The plump wife of the Chief Gardener of Pharaoh has already drunk more wine than is good for her. Many of the other guests also are highly exhilarated, but poor Nozme is nearing the point of collapse. She sways back in her seat, laughing loudly and immoderately. Her wig has slipped to one side and her eye-paint has run. The guests near her laugh with her, and a slave re-fills her cup, which almost falls from her hand. No one, not even Meryet, is shocked. One is expected to get drunk at parties. But Nozme always reaches the point of intoxication quicker than anyone else. A slave stands near her, watching her closely, a bowl in his hand.

Now the male singers have retired and a new group of musicians enters. This time the instrumentalists are young girls, clad in little but fringed loin-cloths and a few beads. There are two singers, a young man and a young girl. They go through a few dancing movements, the man advancing on the girl, kneeling with arms outstretched, while the girl pretends to run away. He turns his back, hides his head in his hands, and she comes tripping back. He turns, rises, and sings to her, while the girl accompanists play a plaintive tune on their flutes and lyres.

> "The love of the sister is upon yonder side
>   A stretch of water is between us,
>   And a crocodile waits on the sandbank.
>   But when I go down into the water
>   I tread upon the flood;
>   My heart is courageous upon the waters
>   And the water is like land to my feet. . . ."

A hush has fallen on the audience. They sit, with their wine-cups in their hands, looking sentimentally at the singer

Some have their arms round their companions. In the dark
corners couples are embracing.

> "Her love it is that makes me strong;
>   Yes, it makes water-spell for me. . . .
>   I see my sister[1] coming and my heart rejoices."

Sinuhe, the young son of the Chief Secretary and Tiyi,
is sitting beside his parents. He looks across the lighted
hall, past the singers, to the group surrounding the Vizier.
A pair of dark eyes are looking straight at him, those of
Ta-kha'et. When he returns her glance she looks away and
begins to toy with the lotus flower which she holds in her
slim fingers. But Sinuhe does not take his eyes away.

> "I see my sister coming and my heart rejoices
>   My arms are opened wide to embrace her
>   And my heart rejoices upon its place. . . .
>   When the mistress comes to me
>   If I embrace her and her arms are opened
>   It is for me as if I were one that is from Punt[2] . . ."

The male singer ends his song. There is a burst of
clapping; then the flutes and the lyres strike up again and
the girl singer advances with shy, coquettish movements.
Then she sings to the boy:

> "My brother, it is pleasant to go to the pool
>   In order to bathe me in thy presence,
>   That I may let thee see my beauty in my tunic of finest royal
>   linen
>   When it is wet. . . .
>   I go down with you into the water.
>   And come forth again with a red fish
>   Which lies beautiful on my fingers.
>   Come and look at me. . . ."

[1] In Egyptian love-songs the words "sister" and "brother" simply mean
"beloved" and do not necessarily denote blood relationship.
[2] The land of perfumes.

But at this point there is a sudden uproar. Nozme has slipped from her chair. Her husband helps her to her feet, when she has a swift attack of nausea. Some of the nearby guests laugh. A slave rushes forward with a bowl. Nozme lunges forward, misses her footing, and sprawls across the floor, knocking over the charcoal brazier which stands at the end of the room to give warmth (for the night has now grown cold). The glowing coals scatter across the floor. One of the ladies screams and draws back, upsetting her chair. The slaves rush forward, and so do some of the guests, including Sinuhe, whose parents do not notice his absence in the confusion. But Sinuhe is not interested in putting out the fire. He reaches the pillar which screens him from the Vizier and his wife. Ta-kha'et, who has also darted out to watch the scene, is suddenly beside him. Without a word he takes her in his arms and kisses her. It is all over in a second. She struggles from his grasp and returns to her parents, while the young man goes slowly back to his chair on the other side of the hall. But it is all right. Even Tiyi has not noticed anything.

But one person has noticed—Nofret, Ta-kha'et's elder sister. She is sitting a little apart from her parents, surrounded by other young girls of good family, with whom she has spent the entire evening discussing dress, court gossip, and men. Unlike her companions, Nofret is not greatly interested in men as such; only in the offices they hold. It is not that she is mercenary; she has no need to be. She is the daughter of the Vizier and a priestess of Amun privileged to walk before the Pharaoh himself when he enters the Temple of the King of Gods. All her life she has been surrounded by the high officers of the King, the chosen instruments of the royal power. When she marries, as, sooner or later she must, it will be to some such official;[1] he will be a great man, and her children, when she has them, will be destined also for high office. That is why the action

---

[1] Warning to romantics. He could be her brother, or even her father.

of Ta-kha'et puzzled her. Sinuhe, who was he? A handsome youth, of good family, not without talent, but of small
account in the affairs of state. She could have had twenty
such; men like Senmut over there, the young officer of
charioteers, looking at her with his melancholy eyes. The
fool! Who ever heard of a Vizier's daughter marrying a
mere Army officer?

As for love, the concubines looked after that, women
like Mutardis, her father's chief favourite. And at that
moment the dancer enters, accompanied by a group of
lovely young girls, naked except for brief loin-cloths and the
beaded ornaments which adorn their breasts, arms and
ankles. Some carry tambourines, others lutes. They wear
flowers in their dark hair, and their eyes are heavily painted.

The guests clap and lean forward in their chairs, as
Mutardis herself glides into the centre of the hall. She is
about thirty, and her skin is darker than that of most of her
companions, for she has Nubian blood. Her black wig,
falling to her shoulders, frames a mask-like face of im-
passive beauty. Even during her most voluptuous movements her expression never changes; rapt and expression-
less, it seems to be no part of the provocation of her body.
She dances with slow, serpentine movements, weaving her
hips to the rhythm of the music, accenting it occasionally
with a clack-clack of the castanets which she holds in her
hands. She flings back her head, letting the black curls hang,
then flings them forward over her eyes. Her arms outstretched, she sinks to her knees, then slowly rises again
with a vibrating movement of her whole body. Meanwhile,
the chorus of girls sings an ancient song:

"Sweet of love is the daughter of the King!
  Black are her tresses as the blackness of the night,
  Black as the wine-grapes are the clusters of her hair,
  The hearts of the women turn towards her with delight,
  Gazing on her beauty with which none can compare,

"Sweet of love is the daughter of the King!
Fair are her arms in the softly swaying dance,
Fairer by far is her bosom's rounded swell!
The hearts of the men are as water at her glance,
Fairer is her beauty than mortal tongue can tell. . . ."

Rekhmire watches, leaning forward in his chair, intent. Tiyi remarks to her meek husband, "One would never think she had had four children by him." Senmut, his chin resting on his cupped hands, remembers a dancer he knew in Kadesh. Nofret looks on, detached and indifferent. This was the sort of thing which men liked.

"Sweet of love is the daughter of the King!
Rose are her cheeks as the jasper's ruddy hue,
Rose as the henna which stains her slender hands!
The heart of the King is filled with love anew,
When in all her beauty before his throne she stands."[1]

The dance is over. With a final frenzy of castanets and drums, Mutardis glides backwards out of the hall, her head bowed, her black curls falling over her face. The guests stamp and clap their hands. Nozme almost falls off her chair again and is saved by her husband. Meryet looks at her husband, who smiles and looks away.

And now it is near the end of the feast. Led by two young slaves, an aged harper enters the hall, bowing to right and left. He is blind, and for many years has been in Rekhmire's service. He knows the ancient songs which have been sung in Egypt for 1,000 years. His father was a harper, and his before him. He takes his seat in the place of honour beside his lord, and tunes his instrument. While this is happening, Senmut leans forward and hands to Kenamun the roll of papyrus which he has been holding all evening.

"Please give this to Nofret when I have gone," he says, not daring to look into his friend's eyes. Kenamun slips the roll into his tunic and makes no comment.

[1] Translation by Arthur Weigall.

Now, at the end of the feast, comes the song which has been sung at Egyptian banquets for untold centuries, and which is recorded in many tombs. It expresses all too clearly the inner doubt which the Egyptians felt about the after-life for which they so carefully prepared. The Chief Priest thinks it is a little impious, but Rekhmire likes it. After a few preliminary strokes across the strings, the harper begins:

"Bodies pass away and others remain since time of them that were
     before.
The gods that were aforetime rest in their pyramids, and likewise
     the noble and the glorified, buried in their pyramids.
They that build houses, their habitations are no more.
What hath been done with them?"

A silence has settled on the guests. Rekhmire's mind is far away, thinking of the deserted monuments which he passed on his way up-river; the pyramid of Cheops, of Chephren, of Djoser. . . .

"I have heard the discourses of Imhotep and Hardedef with
     whose words men speak everywhere.
What are their habitations now?
Their walls are destroyed, their habitations are no more, as if
     they had never been."

"None cometh from thence that he may tell us how they fare,
     that he may tell us what they need, that he may set our heart
     at rest, until we also go to the place whither they are gone."

Senmut, hazy with wine, his head sunk on his chest, feels the ultimate pagan pessimism, a pessimism that has nothing to do with his unavailing love for Nofret. Is this all that life has to offer? Is this the ultimate summation of the splendour of Egypt, the achievement of his ancestors, the glory of their monuments? A round of sensuality ending in final extinction? The harper sings on, but his words bring no comfort to Senmut.

"Be glad, that thou mayest cause thine year to forget that men will one day beautify thee.

Follow thy desire, so long as thou livest.

Put myrrh on thy head, clothe thee in fine linen, and anoint thee with the genuine marvels of the things of the God.

Increase yet more the delights that thou hast, and let not thy heart grow faint.

Follow thy desire, and do good to thyself.

Do what thou requirest upon earth and vex not thine heart— until that day of lamentation comes to thee.

Yet He with the Quiet Heart[1] hears not their lamentation, and cries deliver no man from the Underworld."

The song ends, the guests rise to go. They say goodbye to their host and hostess, and, preceded by slaves with torches, make their way unsteadily along the passage which leads to the porter's lodge. There the chariots are waiting, the drivers at their posts, the runners standing ready. The moon rides high over the palm trees, and the torches which accompany the first guests to depart are already a faint glimmer in the distance.

In the almost empty hall, Nofret is reading the papyrus roll which her brother has given her from Senmut. It is an old poem, beautifully set out in hieratic by one of the best scribes in Thebes.

"Seven days from yesterday I have not seen my beloved,
And sickness has crept over me,
And I am become heavy in my limbs
And am unmindful of mine own body.
If the master-physicians come to me,
My heart has no comfort of their remedies,
And the magicians, no resource is in them,
My malady is not diagnosed.

"Better for me is my beloved than any remedies,
More important is she for me than the entire compendium of medicine.

[1] Osiris.

"My salutation is when she enters from without.
When I see her, then am I well;
Opens she her eye, my limbs are young again;
Speaks she, and I am strong;
And when I embrace her, she banishes evil,
And it passes from me for seven days."

Nofret, the open scroll in her hand, walks slowly over to
the brazier and drops it on the glowing coals. She watches it
as it flares up, curls, and sinks in ashes. Then, accompanied
by her slaves, she walks to the women's quarters.

CHAPTER V

THE EGYPTIAN WOMAN

WITH the exception of Rekhmire and his family (whose names are known from his tomb), and Amenemhab, all the characters in the foregoing chapters were invented, but their prototypes can be recognised in Ancient Egyptian literature and tomb inscriptions. All I have done is put them together in a common setting, let them react upon each other, and develop a life of their own. At the same time I can assure anyone reading this book for factual information that he is not being led astray by a flight of undisciplined imagination. Every incident I have described could have happened, and several did happen. The prototype of Rekhmire's house can be seen in Theban tomb-paintings, represented to the last detail: the porter's lodge, the garden, the three passages, the hall of columns, the harem and the servants' quarters, with the rooms peopled by the men and women who occupied them in life. You can see such a picture in the tomb of Ay, at Tell-el-Amarna, and there are other examples. Pictures of feasts occur frequently in Egyptian tombs, and most of the details of Rekhmire's feast have been taken from scenes in his own tomb. There you may still see the musicians, the dancing girls and the guests holding lotus flowers, watching the entertainment while slaves hand them food and drink.

That children sometimes attended such feasts is proved by the fact that one of the tomb-frescoes at Tell-el-Amarna shows the small daughters of Akhnaten and Nefretiti sitting beside their parents' chairs, and even Nebet's toy dog has its prototype, found in a tomb. In another Theban

tomb you can see Nozme getting drunk and vomiting into a
bowl held by a slave; in another a blind harper is shown,
and above his figure is the very song which I have put into
the mouth of Rekhmire's singer. All the songs are authentic,
the love-songs, the hymns to Amun-Re and the song to
which Mutardis danced. Some of these were found on
papyri of an earlier or later date than the period we are
describing, but there is no reason to suppose that these
songs, or others like them, were not sung in the time of
Rekhmire. As for the Vizier himself, and his beautiful wife,
their portraits can be seen to this day in a Theban tomb
which is one of the most interesting in the Necropolis. In
one of these scenes he is shown disembarking from a boat
after a voyage to Middle Egypt. There is no record of his
having visited Byblos, but equally there is no reason why
he should not have done so. Many other scenes from his life
are depicted on the walls of his tomb, and some of these
will be described in later chapters. We shall also meet again
Nofret, Sinuhe and Ta-kha'et, Kenamun and Senmut, in
different settings.

Also it may be objected, by readers who come fresh to the
study of Ancient Egypt, that the women in Rekhmire's house
seem to enjoy a status higher than might be expected in an
Oriental country. In this, however, they would be wrong.
One of the most attractive and human aspects of Ancient
Egyptian life, and one which brings them very close to us,
was their affectionate family life. Among the educated
classes women seem to have been honoured and respected.
Many tomb-inscriptions and many letters which have come
down to us bear witness to the love and respect which the
Egyptian bore towards his womenfolk. One of the precepts
of the great sage 'Eney was:

"Thou shalt never forget what thy mother has done for thee.
. . . She bare thee and nourished thee in all manner of ways. If
thou forgettest her, she might blame thee, she might 'lift up her
arms to God, and He would hear her complaint'. After the

appointed months she bare thee, she nursed thee for three years. She brought thee up, and when thou didst enter the school, and was instructed in the writings, she came daily to thy master with bread and beer from her house."

Another Wise Man, Ptah-hotetp gives the following advice:

"If thou art a man of note, found for thyself an household, and love thy wife at home, as it beseemeth. Fill her belly, clothe her back; unguent is the remedy for her limbs. Gladden her heart, as long as she lives; she is a goodly field for her lord."

However, a man could take more than one legitimate wife, and if he was rich he could keep numerous concubines as well. There are references in some inscriptions to "beautiful singers" and other attendants in "the house of the women". But the chief wife always held precedence; she is shown in the tomb-paintings in company with her husband, feasting or hunting, helping to supervise his estate, or receiving tribute. She is referred to as "his beloved wife" or "his darling", and many of the personal names of women speak eloquently of their husbands' affection; such names as "First Favourite", "Loving One", "My Mistress is as Gold" and "This is My Queen".[1] Another significant fact is that whereas in some Oriental lands the male children were more important than the female (as among the Arabs to-day), in Ancient Egypt the names given to the daughters show that they were held in equal honour. Some of these names are touching; there is "Beauty Comes", "Ruler of Her Father", and—rather oddly—"Beautiful as Her Father". To me the most moving of all is the name evidently given by a father to his daughter after his wife had died—perhaps in childbirth. It is "Replace Her". . . .

Sons also were given similarly affectionate names; "Riches Come", "His Father Lives" and—clearly a soldier's infant son—"Chief of the Mercenaries". Other names which

[1] A particular favourite of mine is "She is Healthy".

could apply equally to boys or girls are "My Own", "I have Wished It", "Acceptable" and "Welcome."[1]

There is a papyrus at Leyden in Holland which contains a letter written by a widower to his dead wife, breathing an affection and tenderness which touches our hearts, even over a distance of 3,000 years. After his wife's death, the bereaved husband was struck down with illness. Some priest or magician seems to have told him that his misfortune was due to neglect of his wife during life. "'Anch-'ere, the dead wife," said the magician, "was angry with her husband, and he must write her a letter to propitiate her grieved spirit." The widower, who was probably a good husband, responded to this cruel advice by writing a letter full of bewilderment, pain and love:

"What evil have I done to you, that I should find myself in this wretched state? What then have I done to you, that you should lay your hand upon me, when no evil was done to you? You became my wife when I was young, and I was with you. I was appointed to all manner of offices, and I was with you. I did not forsake you or cause your heart any sorrow. . . . Behold, when I commanded the foot-soldiers of Pharaoh, together with his chariot force, I did cause you to come that they might fall down before you, and they brought all manner of good things to present to you. . . . When you were ill with the sickness which afflicted you, I went to the Chief Physician and he made you your medicine, he did everything that you said he should do. When I had to accompany Pharaoh on his journey to the south, my thoughts were with you, and I spent those eight months without caring to eat or drink. When I returned to Memphis, I besought Pharaoh and betook myself to you, and I greatly mourned for you with the people of my house.

Evidently 'Anch'ere died while her husband was on foreign service.

[1] However, other names suggest considerably less joy at the arrival of the offspring; e.g. Kison ("Another Brother!"); Nenneka ("No Use"); Nendisy ("I Won't Give Her!"); Entensu ("He's Yours!") and Nehehendisn ("Eternity for Him who Gave Him!").

On the other hand, one must avoid over-sentimentalising the Egyptian's marital relations. He may have been a kind and devoted husband, but he was rarely monogamous if he could afford to be otherwise. Kings and nobles kept large harems, as do some Oriental princes to-day; in the tomb of Ay, already mentioned, can be seen a detailed representation of the owner's harem, with the bored eunuchs lounging at the doors of the women's chambers, the occupants of which are making up their faces, dressing each other's hair and practising dances and songs for the entertainment of their master. Most of these women were probably slaves, and did not find any degradation in their position; in fact, it was an honour for a woman to "find favour in the eyes of her lord". The children of such women were brought up in the harem, but the children of the chief wife probably had precedence. Also the slaves and concubines had no legal status, and could be dismissed at will.

Woman in all her aspects can be recognised in the pages of Egyptian literature; the devoted wife, the good mother, the passionate young girl, the prostitute, the "floosie" and the seductress. The latter type occurs frequently, and warnings against her wiles are given in the Wisdom Books, the reputed sayings of such wise men as Imhotep, 'Eney and Ptah-hotetp:

"Beware of a woman from strange parts, whose city is not known. When she comes do not look at her or know her. She is as the eddy in deep water, the depth of which is unknown. The woman whose husband is far off writes to thee every day. If no witness is near her she stands up and spreads out her net. O fearful crime to listen to her!"

To avoid falling into such snares young men were advised to marry early and beget children, the possession of which was considered the greatest happiness. "Thy wife will present thee with a son like unto thyself."

The high status which "respectable" women enjoyed in

Ancient Egypt arose in part from the matriarchal system, on which the family was based. All landed property descended in the female line from mother to daughter. When a man married an heiress, he enjoyed her property only as long as his wife lived. On her death it passed to her daughter and her daughter's husband. This practice was never more strictly observed than in the Royal Family, which explains why so many of the Pharaohs married their sisters, or even their daughters. Often these marriages were purely formal affairs. A Pharaoh might marry his infant daughter. Margaret Murray, in her *The Splendour that was Egypt*,[1] says:

"The marriage laws of Ancient Egypt were never formulated, and knowledge of them can be obtained only by working out the marriages and genealogies. It then becomes evident that a Pharaoh safeguarded himself from abdication by marrying every heiress without any regard to consanguinity, so that if the chief heiress died, he was already married to the next in succession and thus retained the sovereignty . . . the throne went strictly in the female line. The great wife of the king was the heiress; by right of marriage with her, the king came to the throne. The king's birth was not important. He might be of any rank, but if he married the queen he at once became king; the queen was queen by right of birth, the king by right of marriage."

This custom of matrilineal descent explains the marriages of Cleopatra. She first married her eldest brother, whose right to the throne was thus established. When he died, Cleopatra married her younger brother, who ruled by right of this marriage. There were no children by either of these unions. When Caesar conquered Egypt, he in turn had to marry Cleopatra to make his accession legal in the eyes of the Egyptian people. Next came Marc Antony, who, by marrying Cleopatra, secured the throne. She had a son by Caesar, a son and daughter by Antony. When Antony fell and Octavius arrived, he too was ready to espouse the

[1] Published by Sidgwick & Jackson, 1949.

F

much married Queen, but, as Margaret Murray says, "she wisely preferred death".

Affinity was no bar to marriage in Ancient Egypt. Queens often married their brothers, and sometimes kings their daughters, e.g. Snofru, Rameses II and Amenophis IV (Akhnaten). This was done to maintain the purity of the royal blood and keep the inheritance within the ruling family, but the practice was probably less common among the Pharaoh's subjects. However, even as late as Roman times Diodorus could write: "It was a law in Egypt, against the custom of all other nations, that brothers and sisters might marry one with another." The Romans used to say: "You may go half-way to Athens" (the Greeks permitted marriage with a half-sister), "the whole way to Alexandria."

It is sometimes thought that consanguineous marriages produce mental or physical defects in the children. This does not necessarily happen—in fact, the practice can improve the stock. The trouble occurs when, after generations of in-breeding, a defect in either parent may result in a deformed or imbecile offspring. This is probably what happened at the end of the Eighteenth Dynasty. The "heretic Pharaoh" Akhnaten, though intellectually brilliant, was physically malformed, and his successor, Tutankhamun, died while still a youth.

The custom of female inheritance gave the women of Egypt considerable power.

"The ancestors," writes Petrie, "are always traced farther back in the female than the male line. The father was only the holder of office, the mother was the family link. . . . The same in respect of property; that goes through the *nebt per*, the mistress of the house; we never find a *neb per* or master of the house."

Marriage contracts which have survived show that the woman's rights were well respected.

In a contract dating from 580 B.C., but probably based on earlier contracts, the prospective husband takes oath that if he leaves his wife "either from dislike, or preferring another (apart from the great crime which is found in women)", he will return the dowry and a share of all paternal and maternal property for the children which she may bear.

Another marriage contract, somewhat later in date, contains the lines: "I establish thee as wife. If I neglect thee, or take any other wife than thee, I shall give thee" (here follows a sum of money). The same contractor agrees that half his father's property, which his mother gave him "and the rest of the contracts coming from her . . . shall belong to thee, as well as the ensuing rights".[1]

If the marriage failed, divorce was easy. The formula for the man was to say before duly accredited witnesses, "I have abandoned thee as wife. I am removed from thee. I have no claim on earth upon thee. I have said unto thee, 'Make for thyself a husband in any place to which thou shalt go.' " At the same time, financial provision had to be made for the divorced wife. Similarly, a wife wishing to divorce her husband also had to pay compensation:

"If she shall stand up in the congregation and shall say, 'I divorce my husband,' the price of divorce shall be on her head; she shall return to the scales and weigh for Ashor [the husband] five shekels, and all which I have delivered into her hand she shall give back, and she shall go away withersoever she will."[2]

There is no evidence that marriage was ever regarded as indissoluble, or that any religious ceremony was connected with it. It was purely a civil contract, with a heavy fine imposed on the person breaking it.

As in most countries at most times, marriage, child-bearing and home-making were the principal occupations of Egyptian women. The few professions open to them were the priesthood, midwifery, dancing and mourning. Young

[1] Petrie, *Social Life in Ancient Egypt*.
[2] Marriage contract between Jews living at Elephantine, in Upper Egypt, in 442 B.C. (Petrie's translation).

women entering the priesthood had to learn the sacred songs and dances, but this was not a religious vocation as we understand the term, and they were under no vows of celibacy. Secular dancers belonged to a highly skilled professional class, probably drawn from a lower level of society than that of the temple dancers. Mourning is still a recognised profession in Egypt. In the country, during a funeral, professional mourners with dishevelled hair run weeping beside the coffin as it is carried to the grave, sending up the old, wailing cry for the dead which may have descended from the time of the Pharaohs. These women too would be of the lower class.

Inevitably, when we try to present a picture of Egyptian womanhood, our view will be incomplete, since only the wives and daughters of the well-to-do have left us their portraits. The masses must for ever remain anonymous. We see them occasionally as tiny figures in the tomb-painting of some great noble, working in the fields, gleaning corn (and quarrelling over the gleanings: in one picture two girls are shown pulling each other's hair), dancing for their lord, or mourning his death. Occasionally we find statuettes of women grinding corn between stone querns, just as their descendants do to-day. The life of the Egyptian peasant woman was a hard round of menial toil, regularly but briefly interrupted by childbirth, as in the East to-day. Unlike her richer sisters, she probably aged very quickly and died at a comparatively early age. Occasionally such a woman might see her son rise to high office (for this was possible in Egypt), and then she and her husband might enjoy some comfort and security in their old age—might even be given a tomb instead of a nameless grave. But for the great majority "it is as if they had never been."

The Ancient Egyptians have left no novels, and their histories are mainly dull chronicles of wars and conquests; we shall look in vain for the character sketches of Egyptian women such as enable us to picture a Zenobia, an Aspasia or a Poppaea. Cleopatra lives in the pages of Plutarch, but she was a Ptolemy, and her blood owed as much to the chieftains of Macedonia as to the daughters of the Nile. The women of Ancient Egypt are even more baffling than the rest of their sex, since so little is known about them. And yet so long as the lovely portrait head of Nefretiti exists men will never cease to wonder and speculate. How amused these ladies would be if they knew that after 3,000 4,000, 5,000 years they could still arouse admiration!

Perhaps part of the secret of their charm is the fact that, after many revolutions in the male conception of female beauty, the Ancient Egyptian woman approximates more closely to the current feminine ideal than the beauties of classical, medieval, and Renaissance times. The slim fifteenth-century ladies with their tiny waists and narrow, flowing skirts conform to modern fashion, but their faces are cold and remote; they clasp missals in their slim hands and their thoughts seem to be set above earthly things. The Rubensesque women of the seventeenth century, exposing masses of generous flesh, are perhaps a little too lusty and earthy for our jaded palates. The beauties of Greece and Rome arouse our admiration, but do not excite us. They seem as cold as the marble from which they are hewn. But put Nefretiti in a Dior gown and she could enter a fashionable restaurant and be instantly accepted. Even her make-up would not arouse comment.

But, much as I admire Nefretiti, my own personal favourites are represented in two pictures which hang in the room in which I write, and are reproduced in this book. The first is the lovely frieze of young girls going in procession before Pharaoh, found by Zakaria Goneim in the tomb of Kheruef, a noble of the Eighteenth Dynasty. One of these girls could have been Nofret. The picture is reproduced opposite p. 64. The other, shown opposite p. 66, represents a goddess, and stands in the Egyptian Museum in Cairo. Every time I visit this Museum I always make a point of studying this lovely piece of sculpture. I do not know who she is: I have never bothered to find out. But to me, who am only one among her many admirers, she represents the type of Egyptian woman of whom some long-dead admirer wrote:

"She is profitable of speech, agreeable in her conversation, of good counsel in her writings; all that passes her lips is like the work of the Goddess of Truth, a perfect woman, greatly praised in her city, giving the hand to all, saying that which is good, repeating what one loves, giving pleasure to all, nothing evil has ever passed her lips, most beloved by all. . . ."

CHAPTER VI

LOVERS AND FRIENDS

IT is not difficult to draw appropriate parallels between
life in Ancient Egypt and life at the present day. None
the less, we must admit, if we are honest, that the career
of an Egyptian lawyer or administrator was not exactly
like that of his modern counterpart, nor was the life of an
Egyptian soldier campaigning in Syria precisely like that
of a G.I. in Korea or a British infantryman in Malaya. But
there is one important human activity we share with the
Ancient Egyptians which draws us so close to them that the
centuries melt away; and that is love. The passion and
tenderness of Egyptian love-poems can still move sympathetic hearts, though the warm limbs which inspired
them have long crumbled to dust, and scholars now
ponder over lines which were written only for the eyes
of lovers.

Ta'kha'et and Sinuhe could meet only rarely, and then
usually under parental supervision. But young people
can always find ways of meeting, and the love-poems
which have come down to us betray a knowledge of human
passion which is recognisable immediately by anyone who
has been in love. However, for the moment we will assume
that they are separated. The young girl, Ta'kha'et, is
entertaining some of her friends in the garden of her
parents' house. They lie under the sycamore trees beside
a shady pool while slaves serve them with food and drink
and others sing and dance for their entertainment. Ta'kha'et,
in a fine linen gown, a garland of flowers around her
shoulders, reclines lazily on one elbow listening to the
song, which is called "The Flowers in the Garden":

"*Mekmekh*-flowers! Thou makest the heart equable. I do unto thee that which thou desireth, when I am in thine arms.

"My chief request is paint for mine eye, and my seeing thee is light for mine eyes. I nestle close to thee, because I see thy love, thou man, for whom most I crave.

"How pleasant is mine hour! Might an hour only become for me eternity, when I sleep with thee. Thou didst lift up mine heart . . . when it was night.

"*Seamu*-flowers are in it! One is made great in their presence. I am thy first sister.[1]

"I am unto thee like a garden, which I have planted with flowers and all manner of sweet-smelling herbs.

"Pleasant is the channel in it, which thine hand hath digged, at the cooling of the north wind. The beautiful place where I walk about, when thine hand resteth in mine, and mine heart is satisfied with joy, because we walk together.

"*Shedeh* is it, my hearing of thy voice, and I live because I hear it. Whenever I see thee, it is better for me than food and drink.

"*Zait*-flowers are in it! I take thy chaplets, when thou comest drunken and thou liest on thy bed. I will stroke thy feet. . . ."

The guests show their appreciation as the song ends. Slaves re-fill the wine-cups, and another singer begins her song. She takes the part of a sycamore-tree, talking to the maiden who lies beneath its shade:

"The little sycamore, which she hath planted with her hand, it moveth its mouth to speak. The whispering of its leaves is as sweet as refined honey. How charming are its pretty branches, verdant as. . . . It is laden with *neku*-fruits, that are redder than jasper. Its leaves are like unto malachite, and are . . . as glass. . . .

"It slippeth a letter into the hand of a little maid, the daughter of its chief gardener, and maketh her run to the beloved: 'Come, and pass the time in the midst of thy maiden! The garden is in its

---

[1] I.e. "beloved".

day. There are bowers and shelters there for thee. My gardeners are glad and rejoice when they see thee. Send thy slaves ahead of thee, supplied with utensils. Of a truth one is already drunken when one hasteneth to thee, ere one hath yet drunken! But the servants come from thee with their vessels, and bring beer of every sort and all manner of mixed loaves, and many flowers of yesterday and to-day, and all manner of refreshing fruit.

" 'Come, and spend the day in merriment, and to-morrow, and the day after, three whole days, and sit in my shadow.'

"Her lover sitteth on her right hand. She maketh him drunken, and heedeth all he saith. The feast is disordered with drunkenness, and she stayeth on with her brother.[1]

"But I am discreet, and speak not of what I see. I will say no word. . . ."

Meanwhile, in his father's house, Sinuhe, who, like all educated Egyptian men, has learned to read, is engrossed in a roll of papyrus. He is studying for the priesthood, and his sharp-eyed father, who is at the moment resting on his bed under the colonnade, thinks that his son is studying the sacred writings. He would probably be outraged if he could see what Sinuhe is actually reading:

"If I kiss her and her lips are open, I am happy even without beer. . . . I say to you (a handmaiden), 'Put the finest linen between her limbs, make not her bed with royal linen, and beware of white linen. Adorn her couch with . . . and sprinkle it with *tishepes* oil.'

"Ah, would I were her Negress that is her handmaid, then would I behold the colour of her limbs.

"Ah, would I were the washerman. . . . In a single month I would wash out the unguents which are in her clothing.

"Ah, would I were her signet ring which is on her finger. . . ."

The sun is sinking, the shadows of the trees in Ta'kha'et's

[1] I.e. "beloved".

garden grow longer, and a breeze has sprung up, faintly rippling the surface of the ornamental pool. The sound of lutes and harps comes faintly across the water, mingled with the chatter and laughter of the young girls. Now a girl is singing a duet with a male singer. First, the girl sings:

"If thou desireth to caress my thigh, my breast will comfort thee.

"Wilt thou go away because thou has besought thee of eating? Art thou a glutton?

"Wilt thou go away and clothe thyself? But I have a sheet.

"Wilt thou go away because thou art thirsty? Take to thee my breast; what it hath overfloweth for thee.

"The love of thee penetrateth my body . . . like the love-apple. . . ."

The young man replies:

"Her breast is one with love-apples. Her brow is the bird-trap of Meru-wood, and I am the goose which is snared by the worm."

And his partner again takes up the song:

"Hath not mine heart compassion on thy love for me? I will not let go of thy love, even if I am beaten . . . as far as the land of Palestine with shebet and clubs, and unto the land of Ethiopia with palm-ribs, as far as the hill with sticks, and unto the field with cudgels. I will not heed their designs, so as to forsake love. . . ."

However, not all the youth of Thebes is spending its time reading or listening to love-poems in the secluded gardens of the great. For example, Kenamun, the son of Rekhmire, has obtained his father's permission to go on a hunting party with his friend Senmut and a number of other young noblemen. The party set out several days ago for the hunting-grounds in the high desert behind the

Theban hills. For the past two nights they have pitched their tents in the desert and marched during the day, and now they are arrived at the place where they hope to find sport. Lions and leopards are known to inhabit the district, but Senmut is doubtful if they will be found. "If we find a few gazelle or an ibex," he says, "we shall be lucky."

Kenamun, the younger man, is more optimistic, but in any case he is less interested in a successful day's hunting than in being able to talk to Senmut, the young officer of chariotry, whom he hero-worships. In the early morning as the rising sun reddens the desert sand, they wait near a low ridge, while the beaters erect a light network of fences into which they will drive the game. The two young men sit opposite each other on the ground, Kenamun admiringly fingering Senmut's great bow, which he has carried on his campaigns in Syria. Their servants stand ready with quivers full of arrows.

"My father says," says Kenamun, "that One[1] will be returning to the land of the Mountain-dwellers, perhaps in the spring."

"I have heard talk of it."

"May Amun give strength to his arm."

Senmut nods, smiles, but says nothing.

"Why do you smile?" asks Kenamun.

"Because the Mountain-dwellers too have powerful gods."

"But Amun was triumphant!"

"Menkheperre[2] was triumphant. If he had not been the great soldier he is, Amun couldn't have helped us."

Kenamun laughs. "You'd better not let my father hear you say that," he says.

"Or Nofret?"

"Nofret wouldn't even understand you."

"But she's a priestess."

[1] Pharaoh.
[2] One of the names of the Pharaoh Tuthmosis III.

"Yes; but only because my father has made her become one. She's not interested in anything or anyone but herself."

"You're hard on your sister, Kenamun."

"I tell you you're wasting your time," replies the younger man. "I didn't mean to tell you this, but you may as well know. She burned your precious poem."

Senmut stands up, takes the bow from Kenamun's hands and slings a quiver over his shoulder.

"They're coming," he says, and leaps up the sandy ridge, followed by Kenamun. From the desert comes the distant baying of hounds and the loud cries of the beaters. The two huntsmen, with their companions, wait on the ridge, shielding their eyes from the glare of the sun. Beside each sportsman stand their attendants, waiting to hand a fresh quiver of arrows to their master as the first is exhausted.

Suddenly two gazelles appear out of the haze, racing across the desert towards the enclosure which, unknown to them, had been prepared for their destruction. Senmut grasps his bow, sinks on to one knee and pulls the arrow back to the head. Before he can release it the excited Kenamun has let fly his shaft, which goes wide; the Vizier's son lets out an oath which would have earned a sharp reproof from his father. As he reaches for another arrow, there is a loud twang from Senmut's bow and in a second the first gazelle falls in its tracks, sending up a flurry of sand.

"Try for the second one!" shouts Senmut. But again Kenamun's arrow fails to reach its mark.

"You'll have to shoot better than that in Syria!" laughs his friend.

Together they hurry down the slope with the other sportsmen as, from the north, a cloud of sand races towards them, a cloud which gradually splits into thirty or forty scurrying shapes: a group of terrified animals—ibexes, gazelles, hares—which are fleeing before the approaching hounds.

The bowstrings hum, the long arrows soar through the

air; there is a babel of excited voices, of huntsmen, beaters, and servants encouraging their masters, all mixed with the loud baying of the hounds.

Seven more gazelles lie lifeless on the sand. A wounded ibex stumbles towards the ridge, an arrow in its flank, but is despatched by another shaft from Kenamun; the first time he has hit anything.

Suddenly Senmut hands his bow to his servant with a look of disgust.

"I'm sick of this," he says to Kenamun. "We'll go back to the camp."

Without a word, but looking curiously at his friend, Kenamun mounts his chariot and follows Senmut.

Gradually the sound of the huntsmen and hounds fades into silence, and there is nothing but the padding of hooves on the sand, and the hard breathing of the horses. They reach the group of tents in a *wadi*, and dismount. Then Senmut speaks:

"It's true—that rumour you heard. Menkheperre *is* returning to Syria."

"When?"

"In about two months, perhaps less."

"Are you going?"

"Yes. And so are you."

Before Kenamun can express his delight, Senmut hurries on: "Your father knows about it; he'll tell you in due course. The General has won him over; you're to be transferred to my regiment. But don't think it is going to be another hunting party. You'll have to learn to march for days with little food and water; you must learn how to handle a chariot on mountain tracks. You'll have to fight an enemy whom you rarely see, an enemy who lurks behind rocks, who suddenly swoops down on you from the mountains when you're in column of route, kills a few score of your men and then disappears before you can fit an arrow into your bow."

"But you've fought the Bedouin many times," objects Kenamun, "and you're still alive."

"Perhaps I've been lucky. And I'd rather be killed by them than captured. I've seen what they do to their prisoners. . . ."

"Then why do you want to go back to Syria? And you *do* want to go back. I know that."

Senmut thinks for a while, frowning.

"I don't think it's only the fighting," he says. "Yes; I enjoy that, too—the adventure of it, the danger. But it's more than that. I love the mountains, the strange people, the strange trees, the strange gods. And some of their women are very beautiful."

He reflects again, and goes on: "No; it's not even that. You'll only understand what I mean when you leave Egypt. Once you've been out of your own land things are never the same again. Egyptians who have always stayed at home have no curiosity about life. They think that Egypt is the world. It's not the world. The world is a much stranger place than they can ever know. Wait till you see Kadesh and Tubikhi. Wait till you see the road to Meger."[1]

"Where is that?"

"In the mountains. There the sky is dark even by day. There are oaks and cypresses and cedars which blot out the sky. There are lions and panthers and hyenas to hunt—not harmless gazelles. There's the Pass of Megiddo, a ravine 2,000 cubits deep, filled with boulders and shingle, with a Bedouin behind every bush."

"Well, I shall be seeing it soon, I hope," says Kenamun.

There is a distant baying of dogs and the sound of voices. The hunting-party is returning to the camp. Senmut gets up, adjusts his sword-belt, then slaps his friend on the shoulder with the remark:

"If you want to live to tell your father about it, you'll have to shoot better than you did to-day."

---

[1] Probably in the Lebanon.

CHAPTER VII

THE PHARAOH'S ARMY

I DO not intend immediately to follow Senmut and Kenamun into Syria, because it happens that Ancient Egyptian records have survived which give a more vivid and authentic picture of warfare in Asia than anything I could invent. I shall quote these records in a later part of this chapter, but first it will be useful to consider the organisation of the Pharaonic armies, not only in the time of Tuthmosis III, but in earlier and later periods. For this information I am indebted mainly to Mr. R. O. Faulkner, and readers who wish for further details should refer to his interesting article, "Egyptian Military Organisation" in Volume 39 of the *Journal of Egyptian Archaeology*.

During the Old Kingdom, when war impended, "local officials were called upon to embody and command a quota of troops from those under their authority. . . . The fully mobilised army therefore included a great many local corps of the nature of a militia, the members of which will presumably have done military service or have had a certain amount of military training." In other words the system of recruitment was rather like the feudal system used in Europe during the Middle Ages. The only army unit mentioned in Old Kingdom texts is the "battalion". The size of this is unknown, but if, as the text states, the armies consisted of "many tens of thousands", the unit may well have been the size of a division.

The disadvantage of this system, as in medieval times, was that it put too much power into the hands of the local magnates, and when, for instance, in the Intermediate Period following the decline of the Old Kingdom there was a lack of power at the centre, the provincial nobles made war upon each other and anarchy prevailed. However, there was probably a small standing army as well, under the direct command of the king. Otherwise, as Faulkner points out, it would have been difficult for the Pharaoh to cope with a sudden emergency, such as an invasion or rebellion. Therefore the king probably maintained a small force of trained troops, which were always at hand when immediate action was needed.

In Old Kingdom tombs at Sakkara and Deshabshah there are battle-scenes which give the impression of well-trained and competent Egyptian troops; probably disciplined regular soldiers led the field, backed up by conscripts. Most of what we know of military organisation under the Old Kingdom is derived from the chronicles of a certain Weni, who describes a force levied for campaigns in Asia. Weni does not mention the existence of a regular force but this—

"does not imply that there was no such force. He is simply concerned to point out that all available sources of men throughout Egypt were called upon for service, and he may well have taken the small permanent nucleus of troops for granted as having to service in any case".[1]

It must also be remembered that in peacetime it was usual to levy troops, not only for military duties, but to carry out public works, such as quarrying. The word "general" is applied sometimes to officials who were carrying out duties not strictly of a military nature. For example, of the generals known from the First to the Seventh Dynasties—

"three commanded expeditions to Sinai, three led quarrying expeditions to the Wadi Hammamat, and one . . . was in charge at Turah. Of the others, Prince Kamtjenent, son of King Izezi, may perhaps have seen service abroad, one named Kherdni had

[1] Faulkner.

authority over a whole body of new recruits, while yet another was probably stationed at Elephantine and was in command of Nubian auxiliaries."

The only regular officer whose rank is given in Old Kingdom inscriptions is "general" or "army commander", but obviously subordinate officers must have existed, and indeed can be identified in the battle-scenes at Sakkara and Deshabshah. They carried a staff of office to distinguish them from the rank and file:

"On the Sinai tablet of King Djoser [2800 B.C.] the general carries a staff and an axe; in the battle-scene at Deshabshah the officer watching the sappers at work leans on a staff and has a dagger stuck in his belt. . . ."

Conscription, which in Europe is barely a couple of centuries old, was an accepted institution during the earliest period of Egyptian history. Five thousand years ago young Egyptians of military age were called to the colours, did their specified period of military service under a local commander, and then returned to their normal occupations, though remaining liable for call-up in an emergency. During their period of service the State fed and clothed them. It is not known if they received any pay. We hear of a "General of recruits" (i.e. conscripts) "controllers of recruits" and the "overseer of Palace Youths and Recruits" —presumably the household troops corresponding to our Brigade of Guards.

An important function of troops in the Old Kingdom and later periods was the garrisoning of the fortresses and blockhouses which guarded the frontiers of Egypt and the roads leading into Asia and Nubia. Their functions were rather like those of the Foreign Legion in North Africa, and the enemy they faced—the Bedouin—was the same.

During the Middle Kingdom, after the period of anarchy which followed the collapse of the Old Kingdom, the provincial governors, or *nomarchs*, wielded considerable

G

power, and were allowed to retain their own armies. However, as in medieval times, these probably had to furnish a certain number of troops for the royal service. There was also, says Faulkner, a royal standing army, recruited by conscription, and he draws attention to a *stela* which states that in the year 25 of Ammenemes III an Army scribe "came southward to choose recruits of the Abydos-nome of the Southern Province". On another *stela* (memorial stone) there is a reference to Nakhtsebkre . . . "who gave one man in a hundred males to his lord, the Lord of the Falchion, when he was sent to raise a regiment of soldiers". However, 1 per cent. of the male population can hardly have been a burden on the population.

From inscriptions of the Middle Kingdom we can learn a little more about Egyptian military organisation. For instance, beside the title of "general" we find "commander of shock-troops" and "instructor of retainers". These "shock-troops" were probably picked men used as assault troops. The "retainers", originally non-military attendants on the king, became in time his personal bodyguard charged with the protection of the king's person when he went to war. They were like the "gentlemen-at-arms" of medieval times, and they also seem to have officered the troops of the royal household. There is an interesting autobiographical record by one Sebekkhu, a soldier who lived in the time of Sesostris III, which shows how a young cadet could rise in rank as he gained experience.

When Sesostris III came to the throne, Sebekkhu was appointed "warrior of the bodyguard", with a little squad of seven men; later he became "retainer of *the* Ruler" (i.e. the King), commanding sixty men. He took part in the Pharaoh's Nubian campaigns with six other royal retainers, and on his return home was promoted to be "instructor of retainers", with a command of 100 men. Since only seven of these "retainers" accompanied the King on this expedition, they were probably young officers of high birth.

The administrative side of the Army was looked after by the "Army scribes"; there were many of these military clerks, and one comes across them constantly in records of campaigns. They too had various grades of rank, from the junior who looked after the affairs of a small detachment to the senior who had charge of the administration of a whole corps; their modern equivalents would be found in the Royal Army Pay Corps and the Quartermaster's Stores. But in Ancient Egypt they were also responsible for the conscription of young men liable for service.

However, it is not until we study the records of the New Kingdom, the period in which most of the action of this book is set, that we can find really detailed accounts of army organisation and administration, and, more important, personal records of campaigns, which give us a vivid picture of what it was like to fight in the Pharaoh's wars.

Under the Eighteenth Dynasty the Egyptians became for the first and only time a truly military people. In a way this situation can be compared with the triumphs of the French Army following on the French Revolution and the subsequent rise of Napoleon. After the collapse of the Middle Kingdom, Egypt was invaded by Asiatic barbarians, the Hyksos, or "Shepherd Kings". They were finally driven out by warrior-princes from Thebes, whose successors founded the Eighteenth Dynasty. And with the Eighteenth Dynasty the military glory of Egypt begins. Determined to make their country safe from any future invasion from Asia, these Eighteenth Dynasty kings, Ahmosis, Amenophis I, Amenophis II and the various Tuthmoses, penetrated into Palestine and Syria, subduing the country and establishing strong garrisons there. The greatest of these kings, the "Napoleon of Ancient Egypt", was Tuthmosis III, who extended the dominion of Egypt as far as the Euphrates. Looking at the shrivelled face of this great King in the Cairo Museum (see illustration facing

p. 176), it is difficult to recognise that this was the one
military genius whom Ancient Egypt produced.

The Pharaoh was head of the Army, and usually took
command in the field. The Vizier corresponded to a modern
Minister of War, assisted by an Army Council, to whom he
gave his orders. But in the field the king consulted his
principal officers immediately before an engagement. At
this time too the king maintained a large standing army
which was organised on a national basis and officered by
professional soldiers. Faulkner writes:

"The actual field army was organised in divisions, each of
which was a complete army corps consisting of both chariotry
and infantry and numbering about 5,000 men; at Kadesh [a
famous battlefield of Ramesses II] the divisional commanders
were apparently royal princes, though one division was led by the
Pharaoh in person. These divisions were named after the principal
gods of the realm."

The two principal arms of the service were infantry and
chariotry. An interesting fact is that there was as yet no
cavalry, probably because the breed of horses developed at
that time was too weak in the back to stand up to hard
military riding. The chariot itself was a relatively new arm,
introduced by the invading Hyksos, and was used much as
tanks and armoured vehicles are used in modern warfare
—as a screen behind which the infantry could advance.

"In a field action", says Faulkner, "it was the chariotry which
took the first shock of battle, the infantry advancing behind them
to exploit a tactical success or to stem the enemy's advance if
matters went awry. . . . The chariotry also charged the enemy
at the moment of victory, so as to turn a defeat into rout, and it
is doubtless this phase that we see in those familiar pictures
where Pharaoh charges in his chariot over a carpet of dead and
dying."

The chariots, examples of which have survived in
Egyptian tombs (e.g. the tomb of Tutankhamun), were

light, springless, two-wheeled affairs. Each was occupied by
two men, a driver and a warrior, the latter armed with bows,
javelins and a shield. In this the Egyptian chariotry resem-
bled those described in the poems of Homer. The driver
took a big risk, because he was not armed. His job was to
manœuvre the vehicle into the most advantageous position
so that his comrade could shoot his arrows and hurl his
spears. Two horses drew each chariot. The chariot force
was split up into squadrons of twenty-five chariots apiece
and there were also the "stable-masters" responsible for the
well-being of the horses. As the horseshoe had not yet been
invented, there were no farriers.

The infantry were variously armed. Some were archers,
who also carried axes and clubs. There were regiments of
spearmen, armed with shields. Sometimes these spears were
more than 6 feet long, and may have been used as pikes
were used in the Middle Ages: to present a hedge of points
against a charge. There was also a *corps d'élite* of infantry
known as the "Braves of the King", or simply "Braves".
It was their duty to lead the attack; they are shown storming
the breach in the ramparts of Kadesh when that city was
taken by Tuthmosis III. Then there were special troops
for garrison service, and the famous Medjay, who were
desert police.

Transport was provided by asses, at least in the early
part of the Eighteenth Dynasty. But Tuthmosis III introduced wagons drawn by oxen to transport boats for the
crossing of the Euphrates, and afterwards ox-carts formed
part of the equipment of the Egyptian Army.

By this time too, there was a complete hierarchy of
military rank. There was a special name for privates which
meant simply "members of the Army". The lowest grade
of officer was the "greatest of fifty". Next came the "commander of a hundred" and above him the "standard-
bearer". In Ramesside times (in the latter period of the
New Kingdom) these "standard-bearers" commanded

regiments of 200 infantrymen. There were also names distinguishing volunteers from conscripts, for it seems to have been possible to make the Army a career, though propaganda against the military life was strong among the scribes (who were exempt from military service).

Above the regimental commander came the "captain of a troop" and the "troop-commander", who probably commanded a brigade of several regiments, and higher still in the military hierarchy came the "lieutenant-commander of the Army". There were also administrative officers, such as the "Army scribe", the "scribe of the infantry", the "scribe of assemblage" and the "scribe of distribution".

We owe to one of these scribes perhaps the most impressive personal account which has come down to us of active service conditions in Syria. It dates from a slightly later period than that of Tuthmosis III, but the conditions described by Hori, the scribe in question, must have been exactly like those which Senmut and Kenamun encountered when they followed Menkheperre into Syria.

Hori was an official, evidently with great experience of Syrian campaigning, and his letter is addressed to one of his subordinates, Amenemope, a "scribe in command of the Army"—evidently an administrative officer responsible for food and supplies for the troops. Amenemope, it seems, had "fallen down on the job," and had tried to cover his incompetence by sending Hori a pompous letter in which he boasted of his prowess and attempted to display his knowledge of local conditions.

But every word of Hori's reply reveals the old veteran, seasoned in war, travel-wise and worldly; and yet behind the sardonic phrases with which he mocks his opponent there lurks, I suspect, a not unkind heart. I like to think of Hori sitting in his office in Thebes, his warfaring days over (and he is glad that they are over), yet remembering, not without relish, the days when he "commanded the auxiliary troops . . . the Shardana, the Kehek, the Mashawasha . . ." when he trod the road to Meger, "where the sky is dark by day, and . . . is overgrown with cypresses and oaks, and with cedars which reach Heaven", remembering Joppa, where he had found "a fair maiden that keepeth watch over the vineyards" . . . and who "gave him the colour of her bosom. . . ."

Here are a few fragments of this vivid human document, as translated by Adolf Erman many years ago, and which everyone who cares about Ancient Egypt should read in full in his classic work, *The Literature of the Ancient Egyptians*.

One word of explanation before we begin. Amenemope has apparently described himself as a *mahir*—a word meaning "hero", and this has irritated the old veteran; he returns to it repeatedly in his satirical reply to his subordinate:

"Thy letter aboundeth in thrusts, and is loaded with great words. Behold, they shall reward thee, even as thou look for a load, and shall lay more on thee than thou wouldst.

" 'I am a scribe, a *mahir*,' thou sayest again. There is truth in thy words, say we. Come forth, that thou mayest be tested.

"A horse is harnessed for thee, swift as a jackal . . . and it is like unto a storm of wind, when it goeth forth. Thou looseneth the reins (?) and seizeth the bow. We shall see what thine hand will do. I will expound to thee the nature of a *mahir*, and show thee what he doeth.

"Hast thou not gone to the land of Khatti, and hast thou not seen the land of Upe?[1] Khedem—dost thou not know the nature of it, and Igedii too, what it is like? Sumur of Sesse—on which side of it lieth the town of Kher . . . ? What is its stream like? Hast thou not marched to Kadesh and Tubikhi? Hast thou not gone unto the region of the Bedouins with the auxiliary troops of the Army?

"Hast thou not trodden the road to Meger, where the sky is dark by day, and it is overgrown with cypresses (?) and oaks, and with cedars that reach high heaven? There are more lions there than panthers and hyenas (?) and it is girt about with Bedouins on [every] side.

[1] Locality near Damascus. A Caananite name.

"Has thou not climbed Mount Shewe? Hast thou not trodden it, while thy hands are laid upon . . . and thy chariot is battered by the ropes as thy horse is dragged (?)?

"Prithee let *me tell thee of* . . . beret. Thou shrinkest from climbing it and crossest [rather] its stream. . . `. Thou beholdest how it tastes to be a *mahir*, when thou bearest thy chariot on thy shoulder. . . .

"When thou comest to a halt in the evening, thy whole body is crushed . . . and thy limbs are broken. . . . Thou awakenest, when it is the hour for . . . in the . . . night.

"Thou art alone to do the harnessing, brother cometh not to brother; the fugitives (?) have come into the camp, the horse hath been let loose, the . . . hath been ransacked (?) in the night, thy clothes have been stolen. Thy groom hath awakened in the night and hath marked *what they* (?) *have done*; he hath taken what was left, and hath joined (the ranks of) the wicked. He hath mingled with the tribes of the Bedouins and changed himself into an Asiatic. The foe came to pillage (?) in secret, and they found thee inert, and when thou didst awake thou didst find no trace of them, and they have made away with thy things. Thou art become a fully-equipped *mahir*, and takest hold of thine ear."[1]

Then Hori challenges Amenemope to reveal his knowledge of Phoenicia (the modern Lebanon). Many of the towns he speaks of can still be identified—Berytus (modern Beirut) Tyre and Byblos, and I remember, during a recent visit to the Lebanon, reading this very passage on a hillside overlooking the ancient port of Byblos, looking down on the tangle of ruined walls, some of which may have been standing when Hori and his comrades knew them three thousand years ago:

"I will tell thee of another mysterious city, Byblos by name. What is it like? Their goddess—of her another time. Hast thou not trodden it?

"Come teach me about Berytus, and about Sidon and Sarepta. Where is the stream of Nezen, and what is Us like?

"They say that another city lieth in the sea, whose name is

[1] Probably a gesture of grief.

Tyre of the Port (?). Water is taken unto it in boats (?) and it is richer in fish than in sand.[1]

"I will tell thee of another misery—the crossing of Seram. Thou wilt say, 'It burneth more than a sting.' Very ill fares the *mahir*. . . .

". . . Put me on the way to Hamath, to Deger, and to Deger-el, the playground of *mahirs*. Pray teach me about his road; show me Yan. If one is travelling to Edemem, whither turneth he the face? Turn not back from teaching [us?] and lead us (?) to them!"

Later follows a wonderful passage on the crossing of Karmel, near Megiddo, which many conquerors have passed, from Tuthmosis III to General Allenby.

"Show me how to pass by Megiddo which lieth above it. Thou art a *mahir*, who is skilled in deeds of valour! A *mahir*, such as thou art, is qualified (?) to march (?) at the head of the host! Forward, O *maryen*[2] to shoot!

"Behold there is (?) the . . . in a ravine (?) 2,000 cubits deep, filled with boulders and shingle. Thou makest a detour (?). Thou graspest the bow; thou . . . on thy left, thou lettest the chieftains see *what is pleasing to their eyes until thine hands groweth weary*: '*Abata Kemo ari, mahir naem.*'"

The latter are Caananite words of which the approximate meaning, according to Erman, the translator, might be: "Thou slayest like a lion, O pleasant *mahir*." Hori, of course, is also displaying his knowledge of the foreigners' language, just as a British 8th Army veteran might casually throw into his wartime reminiscences a few words of Arabic—or German.

"Thou gainest the name of a . . . *mahir* [among the] officers of Egypt. Thy name becometh like that of Kazardi, the chief of Eser, when the hyena found him in the terebinth tree.

"Behold, there is the narrow defile, made perilous by Bedouins, who are hidden beneath the bushes; some of them are of four

[1] The city of Tyre lay on a small rocky island.   [2] Alternative to *mahir*.

cubits and five cubits from the nose unto the sole of the foot, fierce of face, their heart not mild, and they hearken not to coaxing.

"Thou art alone, no helper is with thee, and no army is behind thee. Thou findest no guide to show thee a way of crossing. Thou determinest (?) to go forward, albeit thou knowest not the way. Shuddering (?) seizeth thee, the [hair of thy head] standeth on end, thy soul lieth in thine hand. Thy path is full of boulders and shingle, and there is *no passable track*, for it is overgrown with ... thorns, *neh*-plants, and wolf's pad. The ravine is one side of thee, the mountain riseth on the other. On thou goest and guidest (?) thy chariot beside thee, and fearest to ... thy horse. *If the horse falleth down* thine hand[1] falleth and is left bare, and thy ... leather falleth. Thou unharnessest the horse, in order to repair the hand in the middle of the defile; thou art not expert in the way of binding it, and thou knowest not how to fasten it together (?) The ... falleth from its place, and the horse is [already] too heavily [laden] to load him [with it]. Thou art sick at heart, and thou startest to go on foot. The sky is open, and thou fanciest that the enemy is behind thee. Then trembling taketh hold of thee. Ah, would that thou hadst a hedge of ... that thou mightst put it upon the other side! Thy horse is galled up to the time that thou findest quarters for the night. Thou perceivest how pain tasteth."

Hori, now thoroughly warming to his subject, envisages the unhappy *mahir* surrendering to the charms of a Syrian girl and being subsequently detected and taken prisoner:

"When thou enterest Joppa, thou findest the meadow growing green in its time [i.e. when the season is at its loveliest]. Thou forcest a way into ... and findeth the fair maiden that keepeth watch over the vineyards. She taketh thee to herself as a companion and showeth thee the colour of her bosom. Thou art recognised and bearest witness; the *mahir* is put on trial, and thy tunic of good Upper Egyptian linen, thou sellest it [as a bribe to facilitate his escape]. ... Thou sleepest every evening, with a piece of woollen cloth about thee, thou slumberest, and art

---

[1] "Hand" seems to mean a part of the chariot or its harness.

inert. Thy . . . thy bow, thy . . . knife, and thy quiver are stolen, and thy reins are cut in the darkness.

"Thine horse is gone and . . . over slippery ground. The road stretchest out before it. It smashes the chariot . . . thy weapons fall to the ground and are buried in the sand. . . ."

Then the *mahir* finds his way back to his Egyptian comrades, but they do not recognise him, as he has lost his clothes and equipment:

"Thou beggest, 'Give me food and water, for I have arrived safely.' They turn a deaf ear, they do not listen, they pay no heed to thy tales.

"Thou makest thy way into the smithy, and the workshop surroundeth thee. Smiths and cobblers are all about thee. They do all that thou wishest. They attend to thy chariot, and it ceaseth to be slack. Thy . . . are cut aright; its . . . are adjusted. They put thy yoke to rights. . . . They give a . . . to thy whip, and attach to it lashes. Forth thou goest to fight on the field of battle, to accomplish deeds of valour. . . ."

This last passage is, of course, purely ironical, since Amenemope is merely having his chariot put in order so that he can cut a good appearance when he returns to Egypt. And there we must leave him.

The document dates from the time of the second Rameses, and in after years it became a standard school exercise which the young scribes had to learn. The translation I have given is an old one, and Erman was forced to leave gaps in the place of many words, e.g. those describing parts of the chariot, which he could not translate, and also to fill in gaps in the manuscript with conjectural readings (indicated by italics). But I know of no other passage in Ancient Egyptian literature which gives so convincing a picture of the life of a soldier under the Pharaohs of the Eighteenth Dynasty, more than 3,000 years ago.

CHAPTER VIII

PER-HOR GOES TO SCHOOL

THE greatest complex of buildings in Thebes, larger even than the Royal Palace, is the Temple of Amun. Its huge pylons—massive, sloping-sided, which flank the ceremonial entrances—its towering hall of columns, beyond which lie the dark, mysterious chambers where the most sacred rites are performed, the sunlit courtyards across which walk the shaven white-robed priests, the sky-pointing obelisks—all these are only the core of what is almost a city within a city—a maze of corridors, streets, store-rooms, treasuries, granaries, and the domestic quarters of the priests and priestesses, who serve the King of Gods. Among these buildings is a school, and in one of the rooms which we enter now, twenty or so small boys sit cross-legged on the floor.

At the top of the room sits their teacher, a venerable scribe, a roll of papyrus spread out before him, and other rolls at his side. Each boy has in front of him a piece of potsherd, on which he is laboriously writing at the dictation of the teacher. Later, when they become accomplished scribes, they will be entrusted with papyrus, but for the time being scraps of pottery are quite good enough. Later these school exercises will be thrown away, to be unearthed thousands of years later and pored over by scholars, whose task of deciphering the ancient language will be made even more difficult because of the schoolboys' grammatical mistakes.

One of the boys is Per-hor, the youngest son of Rekhmire. Like nearly all schoolboys of every generation, he does not like his lessons very much, and unlike his modern counterpart he has not even the possibility of gazing out of the window, for there are no windows in this room, only narrow apertures high in the mud-brick wall, through which the morning sunlight streams, throwing elongated patches of brightness on the ceiling. However, there are a few compensations; for instance, old Khaemwese, the teacher, is old and rather deaf, so that one can, if one is careful, have quite interesting conversations with one's neighbour, varied occasionally with a game of marbles, the stones being concealed in Per-hor's tunic.

Care is necessary, however, for one of the maxims of the scribes, which Per-hor has had to copy out many times, is "the ear of a boy is on his back, and he harkeneth when he is beaten". And Khaemwese is no respecter of persons, even the son of the Vizier.

Per-hor is an intelligent lad, and most modern schoolboys would sympathise with his boredom, since the lessons consist chiefly of learning by rote, and laboriously copying out set exercises which have been used in Egyptian schools for generations.

Let us lean over his small shoulder and see what he has written:

"I place thee at school along with the children of notables, to educate thee and to have thee trained in this aggrandising calling.

"Behold, I relate to thee how it fareth with the scribe when he . . . Wake up, at thy place, the books lie [already] before thy comrades. Place thine hand on thy clothes and look to thy sandals. When thou gettest thy daily task . . . be not idle. . . ."

Per-hor's neighbour, young Nebamun, son of the Chief of the Granaries, is copying out another exercise:

"I have heard that thou followest pleasures. Turn not thy back on my words. Dost thou give thy mind to all manner of deaf (?) things? . . .

"I will cause thy foot to stumble when it goeth in the streets, and thou shalt be beaten with the hippopotamus whip.

"However, I have seen many like thee, that did sit in the writing academy and that said not 'by God' without swearing, 'Books are nothing at all'. Yet they became scribes, and One[1] remembered their names, to despatch them on errands."

The pessimism of the Egyptian teacher regarding his pupils is bottomless. When Per-hor gets older, and becomes acquainted with pastimes less innocent than marbles, he will probably have to copy out the following exercise:

"I am told that thou forsakest writing, thou givest thyself up (?) to pleasures; thou goest from street to street, where (?) it smelleth of beer, to destruction. Beer, it scareth men [from thee], it sendeth thy soul to perdition.

"Thou art like a broken steering-oar in a ship, that is obedient on neither side. Thou art like a shrine without its god, and like a house without bread.

"Thou art encountered climbing a wall and breaking the . . . men run away from before thee, for thou inflictest wounds on them.

"Would that thou knewest that wine is an abomination, that thou wouldst take an oath in respect of *shedeh*,[2] that thou shouldst not set thine heart on the bottle (?) and wouldst forget *telek*.[2]

"Thou art taught to sing to the flute . . . and to pipe, to speak to the *kinnor*[3] in anen, and to sing to the *nezekh*.[3]

"Thou sittest in the house [brothel?] and the girls encircle thee; thou standest and makest. . . .

"Thou sittest in front of the wench and art besprinkled with oil; thy garland of *ishet-penu* hangeth about thy neck, and thou drummest on thy paunch.

"Thou dost reel, and [then] fallest upon thy belly and art besmirched with dirt. . . ."

Most of the lessons which have survived are admonitory, but whatever the context the scribe never fails to praise his own calling, and to denigrate those of others. To

---

[1] Pharaoh.   [2] Intoxicating drinks.
[3] Foreign musical instruments.

judge from Egyptian school literature the student was subjected to an almost continuous barrage of propaganda on behalf of the craft of letters. In Ancient Egypt the lettered man was an educated man; only by learning the art of writing could a young man qualify for what in modern terms would be called a "Government job".

Beside old Khaemwese, who sits with his eyes half-closed as his pupils write, lies a pile of papyrus rolls, exercises which he himself probably had to practise when he was a boy, and which he has given to generations of pupils. Let us look at some of them.

Here is one warning the pupil against becoming a soldier:

"Ah, what meanest thou by saying, 'It is thought that the soldier is better off than the scribe.'

"Come let me tell thee how the soldier fareth, the oft-belaboured, when he is brought while yet a . . . child, to be shut up in the barracks (?). He receiveth a burning (?) blow on his body, a ruinous blow on his eye, a blow layeth him out on his eyebrow, and his pate is cleft with a wound. He is laid down and beaten, like a document. He is battered and bruised with flogging.

"Come, let me tell thee how he goeth to Syria, and how he marcheth over the mountains. His bread and water are borne upon his shoulder like the load of an ass; they make his neck as . . . that of an ass, and the joints of his back are bowed. His drink is stinking water. When he reacheth the enemy, he is like a trapped (?) bird, and he hath no strength in his limbs.

"If he cometh back home to Egypt, he is like wood that the worm eateth. He is sick and becometh bedridden. He is brought back upon an ass; his clothes are stolen, and his servant hath run away.

"O scribe Ennana, turn thee away from the thought that the soldier is better off than the scribe. . . ."

But, objects the pupil, that may be true of the common soldier, but an officer fares better surely? To be an officer of chariotry, *that* would be a good life! But the teacher has him there, too, and grimly hands out another lesson. Per-hor, as he copies out this one, makes a mental note to pass on its contents to his elder brother, Kenamun:

"Set thy heart on being a scribe, that thou mayest direct the whole earth.

"Come, let me tell thee of a miserable calling, that of the officer of chariotry. He is placed in the stable because of the father of his mother [out of regard for his good family] with five slaves; two men of them are given him as helpers.

"He hasteneth to get steeds from the stall in his majesty's presence. When he hath obtained goodly horses, he is glad and exulteth. [*Like a modern young man with a new sports car—L.C.*] He cometh with them into town, and he trampleth it underfoot with zest. Happy is he when he thus trampleth underfoot . . . [but] he knoweth not [yet] how it is with him.

"He expendeth his wealth which he hath from the father of his mother, that he may acquire a chariot. Its pole costeth three *deben* and the chariot costs five *deben*.

"He hasteneth to trample underfoot from upon it. He maketh himself into one that is shod . . . he taketh himself and thrusteth himself into the sandals. He casteth the chariot away in the thicket, and his feet are cut by the sandals, and his shirt is pierced with thorns.

"When one cometh to muster the troops (?) he is grievously beaten; he is beaten upon the ground, beaten with a hundred stripes."

And once again comes the unvarying refrain;

"Be a scribe, who is freed from forced labour, and protected from all work."

The bewildered youth thinks that perhaps a farmer's life would offer compensations. But would it?

"Dost thou not bethink thee how it fareth with the husbandman, when the harvest is registered. The worm hath taken half the corn, the hippopotamus hath devoured the rest.[1] The mice

[1] Compare the American folk-song, "The Boll-weevil": "The tax-man got half the cotton, the boll-weevil got the rest. . . ."

abound in the field, and the locust hath descended. The cattle devour, and the sparrows steal. Woe to the husbandman!

"The remainder, that lieth upon the threshing-floor, the thieves make an end of that. The . . . of copper is destroyed; the pair of horses dieth at the threshing and ploughing.

"And now the scribe landeth on the embankment and will register the harvest. The porters carry sticks, and the Negroes palm-ribs. They say, 'Give corn.'

" 'There is none here.'

"He is stretched out and beaten; he is bound and thrown into the canal. His wife is bound in his presence, his children are put in fetters (?). His neighbours leave them, they take to flight, and look after their corn.

"But the scribe, he directeth the work of all people. For him there are no taxes, for he payeth tribute in writing, and there are no dues for him. Prithee, know that."

Even the priest is not exempt from forced labour:

"The priest standeth there as an husbandman, and the *we'eb*-priest worketh in the canal. . . ."

The baker is even more unfortunate:

"When the baker standeth and baketh and layeth bread on the fire, his head is inside the oven, and his son holdeth fast his feet. Cometh it to pass that he slippeth from his son's hand, he falleth into the blaze.

"But the scribe, he directeth every work that is in this land."

*   *   *

Poor Per-hor! Did he and his schoolfellows believe all this? Not all of them presumably, since there was never any lack of soldiers, farmers, craftsmen, priests and tradesmen in Ancient Egypt. But it was true that for any young man who wished to rise to high administrative rank it was necessary to master the difficult art of writing. Just how difficult it was can be discovered by any reader who cares

H

to consult a primer of the ancient language and take the first few steps towards learning it. If he gives up in despair (as I did) he will at least come away with an increased respect for the boys who learned it in ancient times, and even more for the modern scholars who, at a distance of 5,000 years, have given us the translations from which I have drawn so liberally for this book.

For it was not an easy language to learn. It began as a system of picture-writing, which served well enough to recall something to the writer's mind, but from which a reader would have difficulty in discovering the desired idea. For instance, to quote from Erman's introduction to his admirable *Literature of the Ancient Egyptians*:

". . . If two people agree that the one is to supply an ox in three month's time, in return for which the other will pay five jars of honey, pictures of the moon, the ox, the bee, and the jar, in addition to small strokes indicating the numbers, suffice as tokens for them both, but a third person would never be able to explain these signs with certainty. This preliminary structure must therefore undergo considerable development. Individual peoples have proceeded on very different lines, and have thereby arrived at all sorts of writing of words and syllables. The Egyptians alone were destined to adopt a remarkable method, following which they attained to the highest form of writing, the alphabet."

Fundamentally the method was quite simple. As the system of writing developed and the Egyptian wanted to write words which it would have been difficult, or even impossible, to draw (because of the number and complexity of the symbols), he began to substitute for such words other words, which could be easily drawn, *and which had a similar sound*. From the context the reader would recognise what was really meant. For instance, the hieroglyphic sign (🐦) the swallow, had the sound *wr*. But the sound *wr* also meant "great"; the reader could easily tell which meaning was intended. Or take the sign (🪲) the beetle, which had

the sound *khpr*. The same sound also meant "to become".
To quote Erman again:

"Since in Egyptian, as in the related languages, the meaning of
a word is attached to its consonants, whereas the vowels decide
its grammatical form, regard was only paid to the fact that the
word which had been substituted for another had the same consonants as it, while the vowels were disregarded. It was if—to
take an English example—'heed' were written with the picture
of a 'head' and 'broad' with that of a loaf of 'bread'."

This explains why Ancient Egyptian presents such brain-
racking problems to the modern translator. The Ancient
Egyptian, knowing the missing vowel sounds, would know,
for instance, whether the word *szm* meant "to hear",
"hears", "is heard", "may hear", "hearing" or "heard".

It is this lack of vowel-sounds which makes translation
so difficult. The Ancient Egyptian reader would know at a
glance whether the *szm* in question was pronounced *sazem* or
sizam or *sezum*, and the precise meaning attached to each.
This causes philologists many headaches, and explains why
they often disagree on the meaning of Egyptian words. It
also explains why, if you pick up a learned periodical, such as
the *Journal of Egyptian Archaeology*, you may be arrested by
a 4,000-word article with the fascinating title, "A Special
Use of the *sdm.f* and *sdm.n.f.* Forms"—and then pass
on hurriedly to "The Report on the Slave-girl Senbet".

So when you read translations of Ancient Egyptian
texts, do not be irritated by those mysterious gaps in the
middle of a particularly interesting passage. It may be that
part of the manuscript is missing, or that, after trying hard
to arrive at the meaning, the translator has had to give up
rather than commit himself to a doubtful reading. Also do
not be surprised if, when comparing two translations of the
same passage, different meanings are given to the same
words. Progress in decipherment is slow but continuous,
and many of the translations which appear in earlier works

on Egypt are now partly outdated. For instance, a scholar
such as Sir Alan Gardiner or Professor Fairman might give a
somewhat different rendering of the passages I have quoted
in Erman's translation.

To return to the development of the language: a time
came when such simple signs as I have mentioned were
transferred to so many words that they were hardly ever
used for special ones; they became *phonetic* signs. Thus,
says Erman, "the swallow is used not only, as in the first
instance, for *wr*, 'great', but also to write the consonants
w and *r* in words like *hwr*, *swr*, *wrs*, *wrryt*, etc."

Other peoples had arrived at this stage in the development
of their language, but the Egyptians went even further.

They used especially short words, employing one
consonant, to write this one consonant. Thus they arrived
at an alphabet of twenty-four consonants. And here we
come to a difficult point. Erman believed that the Phoenicians, from whom the Greeks borrowed their alphabet,
derived theirs in turn from the Ancient Egyptians. A great
many scholars believe this too, notably Sir Alan Gardiner.
More than thirty years ago, Sir Alan, with Professor
Peet, was entrusted with the publication of certain
inscriptions discovered and copied by Sir Flinders Petrie
at Serabit el-Khadim in central Sinai. Among these were
copies of ten rock tablets of which some, in Sir Alan's
words, "were clearly borrowed from the hieroglyphs, whilst
others were equally clearly not so borrowed". Among
these non-Egyptian signs the scholar noticed an ox-head.

"This," writes Sir Alan, "brought to mind the old contention
of Gesenius that the prototypes of the Phoenician letters must
originally have had the shapes indicated by the Hebrew letter
names, and accordingly I exclaimed to my companion, 'Surely
we must here have the origin of the Phoenician *âleph*.' "

He persisted, and—

"to my astonishment, almost perfect equivalents were found for *bêth*, 'house', *mêm*, 'water'—the Egyptians always depicted water as a zigzag line—*ayin*, 'eye', and *rêsh*, 'head', besides others for one reason or another less convincing. . . ."

The total number of different signs did not exceed thirty-two, "and of these some might well be variants; the natural inference was that the writing was alphabetic."

Then Sir Alan isolated a sequence of letters in this hitherto unknown script which occurred no less than six times. Applying his principle, he read the first sign as *B*, the second as ' (*'ayin*)—a peculiar guttural sound not heard in English—and the last as *T*. The third sign puzzled him for a while:

"Running my eye down the Phoenician alphabet in the first reference book which came to hand, I naturally stopped at *lamedh*" (a diagonal line with a hook at the bottom).

There was a similar line in the Sinaitic inscription, but in this case the hook was at the top. But if it was the same sign, then the meaning should be *L*. Putting the four consonants together, Sir Alan read the word *Ba'alat*.

Ba'alat was the Phoenician goddess, consort of Baal.

"The regular Egyptian translation of the Semitic divine name Ba'alat was Hathor (so at Byblus) and . . . the goddess of the temple of Serabit [where the tablets were found] was well known to be 'Hathor, lady of the Turquoise', her name occurring on a large majority of the hieroglyphic inscriptions there found.

". . . Could this be mere coincidence? I thought and still think not. But if not, I had hit upon the origin of the alphabet, for the train of reasoning employed formed a rigid system, and if the conclusion were accepted, it would be wellnigh impossible to deny the premises. In other words, but for an almost unbelievable chance, the name Ba'alat is the true reading and demonstrates a genetic relationship between the Egyptian hieroglyphs, the Sinai characters, and the Phoenician letters with their traditional names."

I have digressed slightly to tell this story, because (*a*)

it illustrates the sudden drama which can sometimes
illuminate a life devoted to patient, unexciting research
and (b) because, if Sir Alan's conclusions are correct, and
many scholars support him, then the characters in which
this book is written owe their ultimate origin, not to
Phoenicia, but to the Ancient Egyptians. From them they
passed, via Palestine, to Phoenicia, and thence through the
Greeks and the Romans to us.

*   *   *

So maybe we are linked, be it ever so tenuously, with
little Per-hor, as he squats cross-legged in his classroom,
longing for the lesson to end, while his tired hand laboriously copies out the words:

"Fortunate is a scribe that is skilled in his calling, a master of
education. Persevere every day; thus shalt thou obtain the
mastery over it. . . . Spend no day in idleness, or thou wilt be
beaten. The ear of a boy is on his back, and he harkeneth when
he is beaten. . . ."

Suddenly old Khaemwese rises, and begins to gather up
his manuscripts. There is a stir in the class, which is instantly silenced by the master. Then the small boys stand
up, and, led by Khaemwese, say a prayer to Amun in sing-
song voices. Then, still under the stern eye of the old man,
they file quietly out into the sunlight, but the moment they
get outside a babel of voices breaks out. The boys break up
into laughing groups; a couple are struggling on the
ground, rolling in the dust; others have produced a ball
which they toss to each other. Per-hor and Nebamun are
racing madly along the sunlit street towards the great
gate, heedless of the warning shouts of passing priests.
They reach the gate, and there, to the surprise and delight
of Per-hor, waits his elder brother Kenamun, standing in a
brand new chariot and trying to look nonchalant. The
little boys gather round, loudly admiring the two sleek

horses with their nodding plumes, and the gold mountings of the vehicle which gleam in the sun.

Per-hor is in his seventh heaven. He is proud of his big brother—proud to know that he has been appointed an officer of chariotry, proud to tell his friends that Kenamun is shortly to follow His Majesty to the land of the Mountain-dwellers. None the less, he is just as capable of mischief as other small boys, and as Kenamun proudly drives through the streets of Thebes, with Per-hor hanging on grimly to the rail, the youngster recalls one of the exercises which he has had to copy out that morning.

And so, above the clopping of the hooves and the noise of the streets, he begins to recite in a loud voice:

"Come, let me tell thee of a miserable calling, that of the officer of chariotry. . . ."

"What's that?" asks Kenamun.

The small voice goes on relentlessly:

"He hasteneth to get steeds from the stall in his majesty's presence. When he hath obtained goodly horses he is glad and exulteth. . . ."

Kenamun tries to box his brother's ears, but Per-hor ducks. Standing as far as possible from Kenamun, and dancing up and down with delight, he shouts:

"He cometh with them to his town, and he trampleth it underfoot with zest. Happy is he when he thus trampleth underfoot, but he knoweth not yet how it is with him. . . ."

Now they are nearing Rekhmire's house. Kenamun has his hands full with the mettlesome horses, to which he is still not accustomed, so Per-hor is free to continue his mockery.

"He maketh himself into one that is shod. He casteth the chariot away in the thicket. . . . When One cometh to muster the troops, he is grievously tormented; he is beaten upon the ground, beaten with a hundred stripes. . . ."

The chariot draws up at the porter's lodge and grooms hasten out to take the horses. Kenamun, laughing, tries to grab his brother, but the boy is too quick for him. At the top of the steps he stands for a moment, jigging up and down and calling out: "Be a scribe! Be a scribe!"

The Nubian porter and the grooms are smiling. With a final taunt of "Be a scribe!" Per-hor takes to his heels. As he races up the path to the house, Kenamun picks up a piece of earth and flings it after the retreating figure. But he misses.

CHAPTER IX

THE CRAFT OF WRITING

THE Egyptians were a practical people. Their great achievements in architecture and sculpture, in astronomy and mathematics, had originally a purely utilitarian purpose. Unlike the Greeks, who admired them greatly, they seem to have had little intellectual curiosity, no love of knowledge for its own sake. Abstract speculation held no interest for them. And yet the Greeks owed the Egyptians a great deal—as they freely acknowledged. Thales, for example, was impressed and stimulated by Egyptian civilisation. What the Greeks found in Egypt was an immense fund of useful practical knowledge, not exactly science as we understand the word, but at any rate, the raw material of science.

To take one example; mathematics, in which the Greeks excelled.

"The Egyptian," writes R. W. Sloley in *The Legacy of Egypt*, "developed a practical system of numeration and could carry out arithmetical calculations (involving the manipulation of complicated fractional expressions) with ease and accuracy. . . . He could solve problems involving two unknown quantities and had elementary notions of arithmetical progression using fractions, as well as of geometrical progression. He was familiar with the elementary properties of rectangles, circles, and pyramids. Thus he could deal successfully with mathematical problems encountered in his daily life. The examples we have throw light on the methods of trading, the feeding of livestock, the raising of taxes, and the determination of values of food and drink in terms of the amount which can be made from a given quantity of material.

". . . Most of the problems deal with the concrete—seven loaves, five men—rarely with abstract numbers. While the Egyptian knew how to deal with particular cases, there is little evidence that he realised the underlying principles. The examples [given in the 'Mathematical Papyri'] employ, for the most part, simple numbers and must be regarded as illustrations of method, model solutions, easy to learn by heart and apply to other similar problems."

The same thread of practicality runs through their achievements in art. The masterpieces of sculpture which astonish us were not created and enjoyed for their own sake. Many of them were never intended to be seen by human eyes. Some were realistic representations of the dead, placed in the tomb-chambers and often hidden from sight, as dwelling-places for the *ka* or spirit. Again, the lovely sculptured or painted frescoes which delight us in the tomb chapels, scenes which illustrate so vividly and charmingly the daily life of the Ancient Egyptians, were not put there for decorative purposes, nor primarily to advertise the wealth and importance of the deceased. Their purpose was magical, to ensure that they had in the after-life all the possession and amenities they enjoyed in this one; the soldier would have his troops, the country gentlemen his farms and estates, and an endless supply of food offerings, even if his descendants failed to make actual offerings at the tomb. The painted or sculptured representation became, by sympathetic magic, the real thing.

Writing began in a similar down-to-earth way. It was a working tool, a means by which a man could communicate with others without having to meet and talk with them, a means of keeping records and accounts, of recording events and of writing down religious texts which, being made permanent, perpetuated their magical powers. Hieroglyphic writing was already well-developed at the time of the first recorded Egyptian dynasty, about 3200 B.C. The earliest examples of these signs are found engraved or painted on stone vessels or other objects. Hieroglyphic symbols were particularly well adapted for this purpose, since they can be arranged to be read from right to left, from left to right, or even vertically, according to the requirements of the decorative pattern. Throughout the 3,000 years of Egyptian history the hieroglyphic script was employed for all religious purposes, such as for inscriptions on the walls of temples and tombs, and for monumental inscriptions of all kinds. But for everyday purposes they were too elaborate; the ordinary Egyptian felt just as we would feel if we were asked to write all our correspondence in capital letters—and the hieroglyphs were much more complicated. So he developed a quicker, abbreviated script which the Greeks called "hieratic", a kind of "running hand". The language was exactly the same, but the symbols were easier to write.

Most of the documents I have quoted in this book were written in "hieratic" on papyrus (see illustration opposite p. 113). The early invention of this writing material also helped to develop the Egyptian written language. Unlike the Babylonians, who had to use baked clay as a writing material, the Egyptians had at hand unlimited supplies of papyrus reeds, which grew in abundance on the fringes of the Nile. The stem of the plant was first stripped of its outermost layer and cut into long strips. These were placed side by side and other strips laid across them at right angles. Then the two layers were placed together and the whole sheet dried and pressed. In this way it was possible to make "books", or rolls, of any length; manuscripts exist which are over one hundred feet in length. In later times papyrus scrolls were exported to other parts of the ancient world—for example, to Greece. In fact, we owe to Ancient Egypt the preservation of Greek literature, since "the vehicle by which Greek literature was preserved and transmitted from earliest times until perhaps the second or third century after Christ was the papyrus roll" (*Cambridge Companion to Greek Studies*).

Very early in Egyptian history the craft of writing, originally developed for purposes of utility, developed into an art. For the Egyptians, like all civilised and articulate peoples, discovered that words have a magic of their own, so in time there arose poets, and writers of stories and romances, who used language for no other purpose than to give pleasure.

As I have already quoted several examples of Egyptian lyric poetry (mainly of the New Kingdom) in the earlier part of this book, I shall devote the rest of this chapter to a few examples of the prose literature.

Long before the invention of writing, there probably existed poetry and folk-tales which were recited and transmitted orally, as were the epic poems from which eventually grew the *Iliad* and the *Odyssey* of Homer. But if the pre-Dynastic Egyptians had any epic poetry it has not survived. There are, however, a number of fairy stories, fantastic tales of magical adventure which later scribes wrote down, which may have roots in the childhood of the race. Judging from the surviving literature, the Egyptian seems to have loved stories of magicians and miraculous happenings. Except in the straightforward and usually dull biographies of officials, or the chronicles of kings and princes, there is little realism in early Egyptian literature. The more fantastic and improbable a story was, the better the Ancient Egyptian liked it. Perhaps this was an unconscious revolt against the restricted, over-regulated lives which most of them were forced to lead.

One of the earliest of the magical tales is "King Cheops and the Magicians". Cheops, of course, was the builder of the Great Pyramid in about 2500 B.C., and the tale is a very ancient one, though the manuscript from which Erman made this translation dates only from the Hyksos period, 1,000 years later. It is a naïve, popular tale, such as may well have been recited in the streets by public story-tellers.

King Cheops asks his sons to tell him stories of the great

magicians of the past. First Prince Chephren (builder of the Second Pyramid) tells him of a wondrous happening in the time of King Nebka, one of his predecessors. There was a certain *kherheb* (magician) named Ubaoner, who had an unfaithful wife. Suspecting that she was having an *affaire* with a townsman, who passed the time with her "in the pleasure-house in the lake of Ubaoner", the magician made a waxen crocodile, "seven spans long", and said to his house-steward: "When the townsman goeth down into the lake according to his daily wont, then do thou throw the crocodile into the water behind him."

"So the house-steward went his way and took the waxen crocodile with him.

"And the wife of Ubaoner sent unto the house-steward that was in charge of the lake, saying 'Let the pleasure-house which is in the lake be furnished. Lo, I come to dwell therein.' And the pleasure-house was furnished with every good thing. Then they[1] went and spent a mirthful day with the townsman.

"Now when it was evening, the townsman came according to his daily wont. And the house-steward threw the waxen crocodile behind him into the water, and it became a crocodile of seven cubits, and it laid hold on the townsman. . . . But Ubaoner tarried for seven days with the Majesty of the King Nebka, *and meanwhile the townsman was in the water without* breathing. Now, when the seven days were passed, King Nebka came . . . and the chief *kherheb*, Ubaoner, *presented himself before him*. And Ubaoner said: . . . 'May thy majesty come and view the wonder that hath come to pass in the time of thy majesty.' *The king went with him, and Ubaoner called the crocodile and said,* 'Bring thou hither the townsman.' Then the crocodile came forth *and brought him*. . . . And the majesty of King Nebka said: 'Your pardon, but this crocodile is frightful (?).' Thereupon Ubaoner stooped down and took it, and it became a waxen crocodile in his hand. . . ."

Later Prince Baufre rises to speak, and tells Cheops of "a wonder that came to pass in the time of thy father,

[1] The wife and her maid.

Snofru, one of the deeds of the chief *kherheb*, Zazamonkh".

The tale begins with the bored King seeking a diversion. He assembles the officers of the palace and asks for suggestions, but none satisfy him. Finally, he calls for the magician Zazamonkh, who says to him:

" 'If Thy Majesty would but betake thee to the lake of the Great House! Man thee a boat with all fair damsels of the inner apartments of thy palace. Then will the heart of Thy Majesty be diverted, when thou shalt see how they row to and fro. Then, thou viewest the pleasant nesting-places of thy lake, and viewest its fields and pleasant banks, thine heart will be diverted thereby.' "

The King thinks this is a good idea, but decides to improve on it.

"His Majesty said unto him: 'I will do this: get thee back to thine house (?) but I will go boating. Have brought to me twenty paddles of ebony inwrought with gold. Have brought to me twenty women, of those with the fairest limbs, and with [beauteous] breasts and braided tresses, such as have not yet given birth, and moreover have brought me twenty nets, and to give these nets to these women instead of their clothes.' And it was done according to all that His Majesty commanded. And they rowed to and fro, and the heart of His Majesty was glad when he beheld how they rowed.

"Then a leader became entangled (?) with her braided tresses, and a fish-pendant[1] of new malachite fell into the water. And she became silent and ceased rowing, and her side [the girls on her side of the boat] became silent and ceased rowing. Then said His Majesty, '. . . Wherefore rowest thou not?' She said: 'It is the fish-pendant of new malachite that hath fallen into the water.' He had *another brought to her* and said: 'I give thee this instead'. And she said: 'I want my pot down to its bottom.'[2] Then said His Majesty: 'Go to, and bring me the chief *kherheb*, Zazamonkh.' And he was brought straightway."

The King then explains the position, whereupon the

---

[1] A hair ornament. She probably entangled her hair with her paddle.

[2] Doubtless a proverb: "I want my right in full, my own thing" (Erman).

obliging magician performs, in miniature, the same act which Moses was to accomplish much later at the crossing of the Red Sea.

"Then the chief *kherheb* Zazamonkh said his say of magic, and he placed the one side of the water of the lake upon the other, and found the fish-pendant lying on a potsherd. And he brought it and gave it to his mistress. Now as for the water, it was twelve cubits deep in the middle, and it reached twenty-four cubits after it was turned back [in other words, Zazamonkh folded the water back like a cloth]. Then he said his say of magic, and he brought the waters of the lake back to their place."

This is only a fragment of the full story, but it will suffice to show the charming, unsophisticated character of these popular tales. To me they suggest an odd mixture of *The Thousand and One Nights* and Boccaccio.

As a contrast, I am going to quote fairly fully from my favourite among all Egyptian stories, "The Story of Sinuhe". This dates from the Twelfth Dynasty, a period of intense literary sophistication, when "metaphor runs riot, and decadent features like a deliberate preciosity are not wanting. One Twelfth Dynasty writer pathetically complains of the difficulty of finding anything new to say, in fact there is abundant evidence that literature was now an art supremely conscious of itself" (Gardiner).

But there is nothing precious in the telling of this story; nor are there any magical happenings. This is the work of an accomplished literary craftsman who knows how to tell a story with economy and pace, how to delineate character, how to paint a scene, to describe action, to evoke pathos. It reads like a true story, which it may be. But whether a piece of history or a work of fiction, it stands on its own feet as a piece of writing.

Sinuhe was a "prince and count" under the great King of the Twelfth Dynasty, Amenemhat I. While accompanying the King's son, Sesostris, on a punitive expedition against the Libyans west of the Delta, news is brought that the old King has died. For some reason which he never adequately explains, Sinuhe is aghast at the news, either because he fears that civil war will break out or because he believes that there is a plot to turn the young King against him. Whatever the reason, he decides to fly. The translation is Erman's:

"In the year 30, on the ninth day of the third month of the Inundation, the god entered his horizon. King Amenemhat flew away to Heaven and was united with the sun, and the god's body was merged with his creator. The Residence was hushed, hearts were filled with mourning, the Two Great Portals were shut, the courtiers sat head on knees, and the people grieved.

"Now, His Majesty had sent forth an army to the land of Temehu, and his eldest son was captain thereof, the god Sesostris; and even now he was returning, having carried away captives of the Tehenu and all manner of cattle without count.

"And the Chamberlains of the Royal Palace sent to the western border [of the Delta] to inform the King's son of the event that had befallen at Court. And the messengers met him on the road and reached him at eventide. Not a moment did he tarry; the hawk flew away with his henchmen,[1] and did not make it known unto his army. Howbeit, a message had been sent unto the King's children that were with him in this army, and one of them had been summoned. And lo, I stood and heard his voice as he spake, being a little way [off].

"Then was mine heart distraught. Mine arms sank, and trembling fell on all my limbs. I betook me thence leaping, to seek me a hiding-place. I placed me between two bushes so as to sunder the road from its traveller.

"I set out southward, yet did not purpose to reach the residence [i.e. the Palace], for I thought that strife would arise, and I was not minded to live after him. I crossed the waters of Maaty, hard by the Sycamore, and came to the island of Snefru, and tarried there in a plot of ground. I was afoot early, and when it was day I met a man who stood in my path; he shrank from me and was afraid. The time of the evening meal came, and I drew nigh unto Ox-town. I crossed over in a barge without a rudder,

---

[1] I.e. the Prince left immediately with his followers.

with the aid of the breath of the west wind, and passed on east of the quarry, in the region of the Mistress of the Red Mountain."

Anyone who knows Egypt north of Cairo will be able roughly to follow the route taken by the fugitive Count. He fled from the army on the west bank of the Nile, followed the river southward to the place where it does not yet branch apart, and there crossed it "in a barge without a rudder". Then he must have passed near the site of modern Cairo, for the "Red Mountain", still so called, is near Cairo, and the quarries are still worked. From this place Sinuhe struck north-eastward towards the frontier, intending to make his escape into Palestine.

"I gave a road to my feet northwards, and attained the Wall of the Prince [a frontier fortress], which was made to repel the Asiatics. I bowed me down in a thicket lest the watcher for the day on the wall should espy me."

He approaches the Isthmus of Suez, passing through arid desert.

"At eventide I passed on, and when day dawned I reached Peten and halted on the island of Kemwer. There it o'ertook me that I fell down for thirst, I was parched, my throat burned, and I said, 'This is the taste of death.' Then I lifted up mine heart, for I heard the lowing of cattle and descried Bedouins. The sheikh among them, who had been in Egypt, recognised me. He gave me water, and cooked milk for me, and I went with him to his tribe, and they treated me kindly."

Sinuhe continues his journey towards Syria, the "land of Retenu", as the Egyptians called it. The writer does not bother to describe the countries passed through, mentioning only the famous Phoenician port of Byblus, which most Egyptians would know by name.

"Land gave me to land. I set forth from Byblus and drew near to Kedemi and spent half a year there. Nenshi, the son of Amu,

I

the Prince of Upper Retenu, took me and said unto me, 'Thou farest well with me, for thou hearest the speech of Egypt.' This said he, for he had become aware of my qualities, and had heard of my wisdom; Egyptians that dwelt with him had testified to him concerning me.

"He said to me, 'Why art thou come hither? Hath aught befallen at the Residence?' And I said to him, 'King Sehetepibre hath gone to the Horizon, and none knoweth what hath happened in the matter.' And I said again, dissembling: 'I came from the expedition to the land of the Temehu, and report was made unto me, and mine heart trembled and mine heart was no longer in my body. It carried me away upon the pathways of the wastes. Yet none hath gossiped about me, none hath spat in my face; I had heard no reviling word, and my name hadn't been heard in the mouth of the herald. I know not what brought me to this land. It was like the dispensation of God.' "

It seems that Sinuhe had reconciled himself to a long period of exile, for he accepts Nenshi's invitation to settle in his land. So the exiled Egyptian nobleman adopts the manners and customs of the Asiatics, who to him are, of course, barbarians. He marries Nenshi's eldest daughter and has children by her. The Chief of the Northern Retenu gives him land and places him in authority over his bravest tribe. And Sinuhe serves Nenshi faithfully in peace and war.

"I spent many years and my children grew up to be mighty men, each one having his tribe in subjection. The envoy who went north or south to the Residence tarried with me [i.e. the messenger of the Pharaoh passing through Syria on his official journeys]. I gave water to the thirsty, set upon the road him that had strayed, and rescued him that had been plundered. When the Bedouins began to wax bold and to withstand the chieftains of the lands, I counselled (?) their movements. The Prince of Retenu caused me to pass many years as captain of his host, and every country against which I marched, when I made my attack, it was driven from its pastures and its wells....

". . . There came a mighty man of Retenu, that he might

THE CRAFT OF WRITING

challenge me in my camp. He was a champion without peer, and had subdued the whole of Retenu. He vowed that he would fight me, and planned to rob me; he plotted to take my cattle as a spoil, by the counsel of his tribe. That prince communed with me and I said: 'I know him not; forsooth, I am no confederate of his, that I should stride about his encampment. Or have I ever opened his door or overthrown his fence? Nay, it is envy, because he seeth me doing thy behest. Assuredly I am like a bull of the cattle in the midst of a strange herd, and the steer of the kine attacketh him, and the long-horned bull chargeth (?).'

"*I am even so a foreigner whom none loveth, any more than a Bedouin would be loved in the Delta. But if that man is* a bull and loveth combat, *I also am a fighting bull and am not afraid to try conclusions with him*. If his heart be set on fighting, let him speak his will. Doth God not know what is ordained for him? . . .

"At night-time I strung my bow and shot my arrows. I drew out my dagger and burnished my weapons. At dawn when Retenu came, it had stirred up its tribes, it had assembled the countries of a half of it, and it had planned this combat. Every heart burned for me; the men's wives jabbered, and every heart was sore for me. They said, 'Is there another mighty man who can fight against him?'

"Then his shield, his axe, and his armful of javelins. . . . But after I had drawn out his weapons, I caused his arrows to pass by me, uselessly sped. As one approached the other, he charged me, and I shot him, my arrow sticking in his neck. He cried out and fell on his nose. I laid him low with his own axe, and raised my shout of victory on his back. Every Asiatic bellowed. I offered praise to Month, and his following mourned for him. The prince Nenshi, the son of Amu, took me in his embrace."

The years pass, and Sinuhe is seized with longing for his own land. At this point the writer breaks into poetry:

"Once a fugitive fled in his season—
now the report of me is in the Residence.
Once a laggard lagged because of hunger—
now I give bread to my neighbour.
Once a man left his country because of nakedness—
now I am shining white in raiment and linen.

> Once a man sped for lack of one to send—
> now I have slaves in plenty.
> Fair is my house, wide my dwelling-place,
> and I am remembered in the palace."

Then follows a moving prayer, addressed not to any particular god in the Egyptian pantheon, not to Amun, or Ptah, or Horus, but simply to "God":

"O God, whosoever thou art, that didst ordain this flight, be merciful and bring me again to the Residence. Peradventure thou wilt suffer me to see the place wherein my heart dwelleth. What is a greater matter than that my corpse should be buried in the land where I was born? Come to mine aid! May good befall, may God show me mercy. . . .

"O may the king of Egypt show me mercy, that I may live by his mercy. May I ask the Lady of the Land[1] that is in his palace what her will is. May I hear the behests of her children. . . ."

The King sends a kindly message to Sinuhe, asking him to return to Egypt, for he has nothing to fear:

"What hast thou done that aught should be done against thee? Thou didst not curse, that thy speech should be reproved, and thou didst not so speak in the council of the magistrates that thy utterances should be thwarted. . . ."

And he mentions the Queen, who seems to have had a special regard for the exile;

"But this thine heaven,[2] that is in the palace, yet abideth and prospereth to-day; *she hath her part* in the kingdom of the land, and her children are in the council-chamber. Thou wilt long subsist on the good things they will give thee. . . ."

Sinuhe gratefully acknowledges the King's message and after so many years abroad, returns to Egypt, and presents himself before Pharaoh. At first he is seized with trembling,

[1] The Queen.   [2] The Queen.

and prostrates himself before Sesostris, unable to speak:

"Then said His Majesty to one of these Chamberlains, 'Raise him up. Let him speak to me.' And His Majesty said, 'See, thou art returned, after thou hast trodden the foreign lands. . . . Eld assaileth thee and thou hast reached old age. It is no small matter that thy body be laid in the ground, and that the barbarians bury thee not. But be not silent, be not silent; speak, thy name is pronounced.'"

Eventually Sinuhe, who is still dressed in his Asiatic clothes, manages to stammer out a few words of thanks and apology: "Behold I am in thy presence. Thine is life and Thy Majesty will do as it pleaseth thee."

"Then the royal children were caused to be ushered in. Said His Majesty to the Queen: 'See, this is Sinuhe, who hath come back as an Asiatic, a creature of the Bedouins.' She uttered an exceeding loud cry, and the royal children shrieked out together. They said unto His Majesty, 'Is it really he?' And His Majesty said, 'It is really he. . . .'"

The story ends with Sinuhe's transformation into an Egyptian again, in a passage which reminds one of the scene in Book VI of the *Odyssey* in which the travel-worn Odysseus bathes and renews himself before going to meet King Alcinous:

"And I was placed in the house of a king's son, in which there was noble equipment, and a bath was therein and . . . Precious things of the Treasury were in it, garments of royal linen, myrrh, and fine oil of the king. Counsellors whom he loveth were in every chamber, and every serving man was at his task. Years were made to pass away from my body, I was shaved, and my hair was combed. A load of dirt was given over to the desert, and the [filthy] clothes of the Sand-farers. And I was arrayed in finest linen and annointed with the best oil. I slept on a bed, and gave up the sand to them that be in it, and the oil of wood to him that smeareth himself therewith. . . ."

He is given a sumptuous house, but more important to an Egyptian, his "Eternal Habitation"—his tomb—is prepared:

"And there was constructed for me a pyramid out of stone within the precinct of the pyramids. The chief architect began the building of it, the painter designed in it, the master-sculptor carved in it, the master-builders of the necropolis busied themselves with it. All the glistening gear that is placed in a tomb-shaft, its needs were supplied therefrom. . . . It was His Majesty who caused it to be made. There is no humble man for whom the like has been done.

"And so live I, rewarded by the King, until the day of my death cometh."

*   *   *

I am sorry that for reasons of space I have had partly to summarise this delightful tale; and also that I have not room for further examples of Egyptian prose literature. I have quoted these few examples only to show the kind of stories and poems which educated Egyptians liked to read or hear spoken, in the hope that readers will be led to the rich sources from which they are drawn—books such as Erman's *Literature of the Ancient Egyptians* and other works listed in the Bibliography.

To my mind, the imaginative literature of Ancient Egypt can bring us nearer to the Pharaoh's people even than their works of art. But a word of warning: though much of their literature is rewarding, a great deal is tedious, clumsy and obscure. I recommend the folk-tales, the biographical romances, such as "The Voyage of Wenamun", the love-poems (which have a lovely lyric sweetness), and the best of the religious verse, especially Akhnaten's "Hymn to the Aten".

But the Egyptians were not a mystical people, and even in their highest flights they never approached the intensity and beauty of Hebrew poetry. If you doubt this, read the finest Egyptian poem you can find on their favourite subject—mortality—and compare it with:

". . . When they shall be afraid of that which is high, and fears shall be in the way, and the almond tree shall flourish, and the grasshopper shall be a burden, and desire shall fail; because man goeth to his long home, and the mourners go about the streets.

"Or ever the silver cord be loosed, or the golden bowl be broken, or the pitcher be broken at the fountain, or the wheel broken at the cistern.

"Then shall the dust return to the earth as it was; and the spirit shall return unto God who gave it. . . ."

CHAPTER X

LABOURERS AND CRAFTSMEN

"I was an artist skilled in my art, pre-eminent in my learn-
ing. . . . I knew (how to represent) the movements of the
image of a man and the carriage of a woman . . . the poising
of the arm to bring the hippotomaus low and the movements
of the runner. . . ."

From the tomb of a sculptor (Twelfth Dynasty).

S o far we have dealt mainly with the educated class which governed Egypt; the great officials, the chiefs of the Army, the lawyers and tax-gatherers, the priests and the scribes. These, the articulate few, have left their written records in self-laudatory tomb-inscriptions. But the inarticulate many, the creators of Egypt's wealth, the builders, the artists and craftsmen, the labourers in field and workshop, remain dumb, save for the few words they are permitted to say in the tomb-paintings of their masters. Even the master-engineers, the men who designed and planned the pyramids and temples, and those who organised and drilled the great labour force which quarried the huge blocks of granite for the colossal statues, the builders of the boats which could carry 650 tons from Assuan to Memphis, have left us hardly any written records of their methods. Hence the question which springs to the lips of the wondering visitor when he catches his first glimpse of the Great Pyramid, or the Hypostyle Hall at Karnak, or some tiny gem of craftsmanship in precious metal; *"How* did they do it?"

Fortunately, from the time of the Old Kingdom onwards, a nobleman loved to have depicted on the walls of his tomb the activities of his many servants. From a careful study of these pictures, together with such

tools as have survived, Egyptologists have learned a great
deal about Egyptian labourers and craftsmen, and the
question "How did they do it?" can, in the majority of
cases, be satisfactorily answered.

One such nobleman was the Vizier Rekhmire, who,
among other things, was responsible for the great estates
attached to the Temple of Amun. He was also, as his tomb
inscriptions show, in supreme control of the great workshops of the Temple, where one of his sons, Mer-y, was
Superintendent. Another son, his eldest, whose name was
Menkheperre-Sonb, was Scribe of the Temple Dues. Using
only these tomb-paintings as our guide, let us follow the
Vizier on a tour of inspection.

*   *   *

It is now some weeks since the army of Tuthmosis
marched out of Thebes on its way to the land of Retenu.
Many young men have followed His Majesty, including
Rekhmire's son, Kenamun, and his friend Senmut. With
the Pharaoh away, the Vizier finds that his responsibilities,
always onerous, are now even heavier, since he is virtually
the ruler of the country in the King's absence. Yesterday
he received in audience the embassies from Punt, from
Keftiu (Crete), from Syria and Nubia, bearing tribute which
the Vizier received on behalf of his royal master. For hours
he had sat on a gilded seat, attended by his retinue, while
the foreigners filed past him bearing their tribute on their
shoulders, and the scribes noted down the names and
numbers of the objects for the records. First the Cretans,
slim, dark men with black, curling hair and a proud bearing,
carrying the products of the Cretan workshops.

"One vase of lapis-lazuli fitted with golden bands and handles
. . . ten blocks of silver . . . one gold dish . . . a lioness's head in
gold . . . the head of a crested bird in gold . . . a drinking cup of
gold with an ibex's head . . . a lion's head in gold . . . a large two-
handled silver vase . . . a dagger in a blue sheath. . . ."

The voice of the scribe droned on monotonously, and Rekhmire, nodding on his throne, might well have asked, "Will the line stretch out to the crack of doom?"

Then came the dark-skinned Nubians from the south, with their characteristic offerings, ostrich feathers and eggs, logs of ebony, gold bars, leopard skins, ivory tusks, and the skins of giraffes. Afterwards came the led animals, leopards, baboons and giraffes, for the Royal Zoo; then came slaves, mainly women and children, to work as weavers in the Temple workshops.

On the day previous to the receiving of foreign tribute he had presided in the Hall of Judgement, for one of his many offices corresponded to that of Lord Chief Justice. That had been even more exhausting, for there had been many litigants and the day had been hot. When he was a younger man, Rekhmire had been proud to receive this appointment and had resolved to live up to the highest ideals of justice. Indeed, he had had these ideals boldly set down on the walls of his tomb, "dispensing justice impartially and seeing to it that the two litigants are contented, judging between poor and well-to-do alike, no petitioner weeping because of him. . . ."

But as he had sat, hour after hour, in the crowded hall, listening to the disputes of the advocates, hearing, in the corridors outside, the voices of other litigants clamouring for admission, he had been conscious of a great weariness of spirit. Some of his minor officials took bribes, he knew, and he had tried to stop the practice. But it still went on. Also it was all very well to "judge between the poor and well-to-do alike," but what if the well-to-do had influence at Court? And Rekhmire had many enemies. Still, he had done his best, and, as a guide to his successors in office, had set out at some length on the walls of his tomb "the duties of a Vizier". One fragment read:

"It is he who hears the case regarding any deficit in the Temple dues. It is he who assesses any assessment in kind for anyone who has to pay one to him. It is he who hears all law cases. It is he who allows reductions in the imposts on places or industry. . . . It is he who opens the House of Gold in connection with the High Treasurer. It is he who inspects the tribute of Byblos. . . . It is he who inspects the water-supply on the first of every ten-day period. . . . He it is who fits out ships according as anyone is fitted for it. He it is who despatches any messenger of the Royal Demesne . . . when the monarch is on an expedition. . . ."

"And the monarch *always* seems to be on an expedition," sighs Rekhmire, reflecting on the number of times he has watched the King march out of Thebes. And he smiles as he remembers a phrase which he has had inserted in the tomb-inscription, a true phrase, but one which had surprised some people:

"Lo, as to the position of Vizier, lo, it is not pleasant at all; *no, it is bitter as gall.* . . ."

To-day is the day of his routine visit to the workshops of Amun, of which Rekhmire's son, Mer-y, is superintendent. The Vizier, who has always worked with his brain, has a great admiration for manual craftsmanship, and enjoys watching the making of beautiful things. He also has definite ideas on working methods, and has described himself in his tomb as "*giving instruction to each man regarding his duties in the routine of all manner of production*". Mer-y does not always agree with him, but then sons always think they know better than their fathers. The chariots bearing the Vizier and his retinue sweep through the ceremonial gateway, and draw up outside the temple workshops. Preceded and followed by fan-bearers, Rekhmire enters.

The workshops are large and noisy; there is a continual din of hammers, saws and drills; and a great variety of smells, of wood-shavings, oil, burning metal and sweat. Mer-y, a tall, serious-faced young man in a black wig and carrying a wand of office, accompanies his father from room to room. They go first to the jewellers' shop. Here are men shaping and polishing beads of malachite, carnelian, lapis lazuli and other semi-precious stones. They use a fine bronze drill for making the holes, revolved by looping a bowstring around the shaft of the drill and then drawing the bow rapidly to and fro. At another bench a craftsman is setting tiny fragments of glass to make an elaborate inlay in a gold pectoral. The stones being used, and lying near the workman's hands, come from many parts of Asia: crystal and chalcedony from the Eastern Desert, turquoise from Sinai, lapis lazuli from western Asia. But you will look in vain for precious stones: no diamonds, rubies, sapphires, or opals.

Rekhmire picks up the gold pectoral and scrutinises the inlay.

"Glass," he says scornfully, putting it down. "In our ancestors' time, my son, they'd have used turquoise and amethyst! *What* an age!" And he walks on.

In the next room workmen are boring out stone vases with a heavy stone drill, worked by a crank at the top and weighted to help the drill to bite. Drills are sometimes of stone, sometimes of copper, but the Egyptians did *not* have a method of making copper any harder than we can make it to-day, in spite of the oft-repeated legend. So there was an enormous wastage of metal when drilling or cutting hard stones.

They pass on to the carpenters' shop. A number of articles have been laid out for the Vizier's inspection: a fan-handle, an inlaid casket for funerary equipment, a statue of ebony with gilt mountings, and a silvered mace-head. Rekhmire fingers the objects, then moves closer to watch the men at work. At one end of the room two men are sawing logs into planks. The log is lashed to a stake and one man inserts wedges in the cut to keep it open. The saw cuts on the *pulling*, not the pushing stroke (see illus. opposite p. 129).

Nearby another carpenter is sawing the planks into

appropriate lengths for the cabinet-maker. Look at the
cabinet-maker's tools. He has a simple chisel, a deep,
narrow mortise-chisel, an axe, an adze (which he uses
instead of a plane), a clublike hammer, a mallet, and an awl
(used, in conjunction with a bow, for boring), a straight-
edge, a bench with a rectangular slot, a flanged square for
checking the angles, and a mitre-block. Any modern
carpenter who found himself back in Ancient Egypt in
1500 B.C. would be quite at home with most of these tools;
except, perhaps, the hammer, which had no handle.

Here a man is heating glue over a fire, while stucco is
being ground with a piece of red sandstone. There two men
are applying the stucco to a box; afterwards it will be gilt.
Rekhmire is particularly interested in a shrine of cedar
wood with decorations in ebony which is being made by
four men. One man is carving the recesses into which the
ebony inlays are to be placed, while his companion carefully
shapes the inlays, smoothing them with semicircular pieces
of white sandstone, which perform the same function as
modern sandpaper. Rekhmire has had a hand in this design,
or likes to think so. His hand caresses the polished wood.
"A lovely piece of cedar," he says, suddenly remembering
the slopes of the Lebanon above Byblus with a pain at the
heart. "I wonder," he thinks "if I shall ever see it again. . . ."

At the same time he makes a mental note to add a phrase
to the scene of the temple workshops he is having prepared
in his tomb.

"This noble, who guides the hands of his workmen . . ." Would
that do? No; better make it:

*"This noble, who lays down principles and guides the hands of his
workmen, making furniture of ivory and ebony, ssndm wood, mrw wood,
and true cedar from the mountain slopes of Lebanon. . . ."*

He is still running his fingers absent-mindedly along
the surface of the ebony inlay when his son calls to him
from the far end of the room.

"Father! Don't you want to see the metal-workers?"

"Of course."

In actual fact, he doesn't, because the day is very hot and he hates furnaces and molten metal. But to-day they are casting the great bronze pivots for the new gates of the Temple. So he enters the smoke-blackened room of the smiths, followed by members of his suite, who walk delicately for fear of spoiling their spotless white linen.

There is so much noise that Mer-y has to raise his voice when explaining the process to his father. Apart from the clanging of hammers, there is a loud, intermittent roaring from several charcoal fires, beside each of which stands an almost naked man, operating a pair of foot-bellows. He leans first on one foot and then on the other, pulling up the deflated bellows with a rope. With each blast from the nozzle, which is fixed in the heart of the fire, the flame leaps and the sparks fly up. The courtiers mop their brows and look unhappy.

On the ground is a large mould of burned clay, made in the shape of heavy top door-pivot and its fitting, together with the angle piece and pivot for the bottom. Nearby stand jars containing copper and tin mixed in the correct proportions. There are seventeen pouring vents in the mould, and the operation is one of some delicacy, because if one man is not ready he can wreck the whole work. But all goes well. The copper and tin are placed in clay crucibles, one over each hearth, and when the metals have melted men come forward and with ordered, disciplined movements at the foreman's words of command, pour out the liquid bronze into the seventeen vents. Each section of the huge bronze gates will be made in this way, then fitted together, polished and finally plated with pure gold. Rekhmire sees another scene for his tomb-frescoes (see illustration opposite p. 128).

In another part of the workshops metal-beaters are working with gold and silver. At the far end of the chamber the raw material, in the form of gold rings, is being accurately weighed before being issued to the smiths. Afterwards each manufactured article will be weighed to see that its weight tallies with that of the original issue of metal. The Vizier nods his approval at this careful precaution against theft.

The first operation is to beat the metal into flat plates, using a "maul" of hard stone. Then from the flat plate the vases are hammered into shape over a stout rod of metal fixed in the ground, the rod being provided with changeable heads—flat, curved, or angular, to suit the work. Where necessary joints are then soldered, the operator holding the part in a pair of tongs and using a blowpipe to obtain the necessary high temperature. (For these and other illustrations of the workshops, see Figs. 37 and 38 opposite p. 128 and 129. Also opposite p. 144.)

Rekhmire and his followers are glad to leave the overheated smithies, but the Vizier's duties are not completed yet. Bidding farewell to his son, he drives to the quayside to watch the unloading of huge blocks of limestone which have been shipped up-river from Memphis. The great Temple of Amun-Re at Karnak is always being altered and enlarged. Every King of Egypt tries to outdo his predecessors in honouring the King of Gods, and Tuthmosis III is no exception. One ship, about 150 feet long, is already moored alongside the quay. Another approaches, the crew slackening the sail, paying out ropes and dropping anchor-stones. In the other ships men are poling their craft along to the anchorage, while a lookout man in the bows marks the depth of the water with a sounding pole.

The Vizier stays to watch the unshipping of one load and then, after a word with the chief of the stevedores, climbs into his chariot and is driven home.

*   *   *

That little sketch, based solely on the evidence of

Rekhmire's tomb-paintings, explains the working tech-
niques of certain types of Egyptian craftsmen at one period
of Dynastic history. Whole books could be—and have been
—written on Egyptian arts and crafts and for those who wish
to study this subject in more detail there are some useful
studies by Petrie, such as his *Arts and Crafts in Ancient
Egypt* and his *Tools and Weapons*, though both these are now
out of date, and should be read with caution. However,
Petrie is reliability itself compared with—

"the statements and theories printed by engineers, architects,
and other technicians, after a brief visit to the monuments of
Egypt, which would never have appeared had they consulted
the archaeologist."

So writes Mr. R. Engelbach, late of the Antiquities Department of the Egyptian Government, in what I have found
the most useful and reliable short guide to this subject, his
chapter on "Mechanical and Technical Processes and
Materials" in *The Legacy of Egypt* (Oxford University Press).
Not being a professional archaeologist myself, I know how
easy it is to be led away on false, though attractive, trails.
Ancient Egypt, unfortunately, is still the happy hunting
ground of a certain type of crank, and unless one is careful
to stick to the best authorities, one may find oneself
wallowing in "lost arts", "occult practices", theories of
reincarnation and all the hocus-pocus which prevents one
from getting at the truth about Ancient Egypt, which to me
is far more wonderful than any fantasy.

Let us take a few examples, starting with stone-quarrying.
Anyone who has admired the great obelisk in the Place de
la Concorde in Paris, or the granite colossi in our national
museums, will have wondered how the Ancient Egyptians
quarried these huge blocks of stone without the aid of
blasting powder, or even of hard cutting tools (for iron
tools were not used until comparatively late in Egyptian
history). Incredible though it may seem, these huge blocks

often of granite or other hard rock—were *jarred* from their native rock by pounding it with balls of dolerite, used as hammers. Sometimes copper chisels were used with a mallet, but copper is a soft metal, and, as the Egyptians were not able to harden it, the wastage of metal must have been enormous.

The method they used for cutting large blocks of granite was to "detach the parent mass first by pounding with balls or hammers, made of some hard, resilient stone such as dolerite, held in the hand, and then by the use of wedges. In this connection, it must be remembered that the pounding ball does not pound or bruise away the stone any more than does the blunt-pointed pick of the modern mason. It jars off pieces of stone by vibration, and the efficiency of the work depends on the quality of the blow; one strength alone does the job; harder or lighter blows have no effect" (Engelbach).

Once detached from the parent mass of rock, the colossal statue was pounded into rough shape by the same method, then levered on to a heavy wooden sled and dragged by hundreds of men to the workshops. (In a tomb-fresco at El-Barsha 172 men were shown dragging such a colossus.) If the workshops were some distance away, the block would be dragged on to a ship, or perhaps a raft, and floated down-river. In the shops men worked on it with tools of ever-decreasing size. Then tubular drills were brought into use, e.g. for the eyes, or the rounded corners of hieroglyphs; if small, they were rotated by means of a bowstring (as explained above) or if large by hand and loaded with weights. "Although no tubular drills have been found," says Engelbach, "the eyes of several statues show traces of them, of graduated sizes, and the bottoms of the holes prove that the metal must have been of extraordinary thinness. The nature of the abrasive is a matter for speculation. . . ."

For the final shaping of the statue, metal tools were used,

but as these were of copper, which could only be annealed to the hardness of mild steel, the expenditure of metal must have been very great. But nothing is known about the material and methods the Egyptians used for giving the statues their wonderful polish.

They also used bronze saws, which could cut hard rock, such as granite and basalt. I have seen cuts over a yard long which imply the use of a saw at least 6 feet in length. Again some kind of abrasive must have been used, but we have no means of knowing what it was.

These methods were used as far back as the Old Kingdom (2780-2100 B.C.) and even earlier.

The Egyptians used several types of stone: limestone, which extends from Cairo to beyond Esna; a very fine-grained limestone, hard and marble-like, from Qâw and Beni Hassan; sandstone; and granite of several varieties, pink, grey and black. Alabaster was also quarried, chiefly from Hatnub, near Tell-el-Amarna. The main quarry for basalt, which was often used for paving the temples of the Old Kingdom, was apparently at Faiyum.

The chief source of supply for granite was Assuan in Upper Egypt, where one can see how the Ancient Egyptians split their huge building blocks from the parent rock by means of wedges. The method was to cut a gallery into which a man could climb. Then, with a hard, blunt-pointed tool like a mason's pick he would work downwards, cutting narrow, vertical trenches, one at the back, and one on each side, leaving the block detached on all sides except the base. The next step was to make deep wedge-slots at the base of the block, and then drive in metal wedges with a hammer until the block split away from its base and could be removed. Sometimes, when the wedge-slots were in a position in which it was impossible to deliver a heavy blow, another method was used to split the rock. Wooden wedges were driven in tightly, then soaked in water. After a while the wood expanded and split the rock. Engelbach

experimented with this method and found the wood
expanded in ten hours.

At Assuan one can see thousands of these wedge-slots,
some of great size. Egyptians of a later generation than the
pyramid-builders, when demolishing their ancestors' monuments, used the same method for splitting the granite blocks
into more convenient sizes. (See the illustration opposite
p. 160, taken near one of the Pyramids at Abusir.)

But long before the blocks were hewn from the quarry
and shaped by the masons other men must have worked
out quite complicated arithmetical and geometrical calculations to establish the volume of building material which
would be needed—for, say, a pyramid of given size—and
the building itself would have been laid out with the
utmost precision. For instance, they measured the angle of
slope by the horizontal offset per unit of vertical height,
known as the *seked*. To cut the casing stones to the required
angle they would mark off 1 cubit vertically and then
set out the *seked* horizontally. Then the mason drew the line
which indicated the direction in which the stone should be
cut. One of the most fascinating aspects of Egyptian buildings is that, in many cases, these mason's lines can still be
seen. Also I have seen stone blocks in the quarries still
roughly painted with signs indicating names of the quarrying gangs which were responsible for them.

Such relics bring us very near to the workmen of Ancient
Egypt. I remember, during my last visit to Egypt, going to
Sakkara to see part of the newly discovered pyramid which
Mr. Zakaria Goneim has unearthed at Sakkara, a building
dating from about 2700 B.C. It was probably built by
Sekhem-khet, a successor of King Djoser, who built the
Step Pyramid, the oldest stone building in the world.
Goneim had excavated a considerable length of a boundary
wall, which had evidently been abandoned and buried after
being built to a height of about 15 feet. Sand had covered
it for 5,000 years, preserving the fine limestone surface.

And on that white limestone wall, the blocks of which looked as if they had been cut yesterday, was a thin red line near the base, indicating the horizontal. The masons had dipped a length of cord in red paint, stretched it, and slapped it against the wall, just as a modern mason does to-day.

Even more extraordinary were the crude drawings—also in red paint, which some of the workmen had daubed on the wall in an idle moment; a lion hunt with "pin-men" pursuing the animal with spears, and a portrait of a Libyan with his long and, to the workmen, outlandish robe and tall head-dress, such a man as they must have seen sometimes hovering on the desert fringes. Standing in the newly excavated trench and looking at these drawings on the sunlit, white wall, I felt as if the workmen of Sekhem-khet had just gone off for their lunch and would be back at any moment.

Although no mathematical documents have survived which apply to the construction of a particular building, such documents as the Rhind Mathematical show the kind of problems which were tackled and solved. Mr. R. W. Sloley, in *The Legacy of Egypt*, cites a few examples, expressed in modern terminology:

"*Problem:* A triangle of given area has the perpendicular height $2\frac{1}{2}$ times the base. Find the base and height. . . ."

"*Comment:* It seems certain that the properties of the isosceles, if not of any triangle, now expressed by the formulae which follow, were known; but it is not easy to prove this conclusion from the material available:

$$A = \frac{bh}{2} \; : \quad h = \sqrt{2\left(\frac{Ah}{b}\right)} \; : \quad b = \frac{b}{h}\sqrt{\left(2A\frac{h}{b}\right)}$$

where A=area, b= base and h=height."

Another example quoted by Sloley:

"*Problem:* Find the area of a circular field 9 cubits in diameter.

"*Comment:* The working (out of the problem in the papyrus)

implies the use of the following rule: Subtract $\frac{1}{9}$ from the diameter and square the result. This is equivalent to a value of π (ratio of circumference to diameter) of 3·1605. The fact that the area is expressed as a square points to the method of counting squares on a surface ruled in squares, in order to arrive at the approximation to π known as 3·1415."

I apologise to non-mathematical readers who, like myself, find this somewhat puzzling. It should, at any rate, increase their respect for the Ancient Egyptians, as it did mine.

A knowledge of mathematics was also necessary to solve problems connected with the supply of material, the allotment of labour, and the feeding of troops or workmen. Let us go back for a moment to our friend Hori the scribe, mentioned in Chapter VII. It was he who had to reprimand his subordinate Amenemope, the "Scribe of the Army", for his lack of knowledge of military matters. In another part of the same papyrus he challenges Amenemope to tell him how to calculate the amount of material needed to build a ramp.

"For see, thou art the clever scribe who is at the head of troops! A ramp is to be constructed, 730 cubits long, 55 cubits wide, containing 120 compartments, and filled with reeds and beams; 60 cubits high at its summit, 30 cubits in its middle, with a . . . of 15 cubits, and its . . . 5 cubits. The quantity of bricks needed for it is asked of the generals, and the scribes are all collected together, without one of them knowing anything. They all put their trust in thee and say: 'Thou art a clever scribe, my friend! Decide for us quickly! Behold thy name is famous; let one be found in this place to magnify the other thirty! Do not let it be said that there is aught thou dost not know. Answer us, how many bricks are needed for it.' See, its measurements are before thee. Each one of its compartments is 30 cubits and is 7 cubits broad. . . ."

Poor Amenemope! When he has to calculate the amount of food needed by his troops he is even more at sea.

"The auxiliary troops which thou commandest number 1,900, (also) 520 Shardana, 1,600 Kehek, 100 Mashawasha, 880 Negroes

—in all 5,000, not reckoning their officers. A present hath been brought thee of bread, cattle and wine. The number of men is too great for thee, and the provision is too small for them; 300 wheaten loaves, 1,800 . . . loaves, 120 goats of different kinds, 30 measures of wine—the soldiers are so many and the provision is under-estimated. Thou receivest the provision, and it is placed in the camp. The army is ready and equipped; so divide it up quickly and give to each man his portion. The Bedouins look on furtively and say, '*Sopher yode*' [foreign argot; probably ironical, meaning 'O sapient scribe. . . .'].

"Midday is come; the camp is hot. They say, 'It is time to start.' 'Be not wroth, O commandant of the auxiliaries. We have yet far to march,' they say. 'Why is there no bread? Our night-quarters are far off.' "

Amenemope, in despair, resorts to beating the men, but they will have their revenge. They will report him to the Ruler.

"Approach thou to give the food! *An hour cometh, in which one is* without a scribe from the Ruler. *That thou shouldst take it upon thee* to beat us, that is not good, comrade; he will hear of it and he will send to undo thee. . . ."

Any officer who has had charge of the commissariat will sympathise with Amenemope. Perhaps it was not due entirely to his bad arithmetic. More likely another regiment had "liberated" the missing rations.

After that slight digression, let us consider the actual construction of a pyramid. Some of the stone blocks weighed as much as ten tons. Yet so fine was the masonry that, as Petrie wrote—

". . . the mean thickness of the eastern joint of the northern casing stones [of the Great Pyramid] is 0·020 inch [$\frac{1}{50}$ inch]; therefore the mean variation of the cutting of the stone from a straight line is but 0·01 inch [$\frac{1}{100}$ inch] of 75 inches up the face . . . these joints, with an area of 35 square feet each, were not only worked as finely as this, but cemented throughout. . . ."

How were these great blocks manœuvred into position and placed there with such precision? I have dealt with this at some length in *The Lost Pharaohs*, but, briefly, the only mechanical aids the Ancient Egyptian workmen had were the lever and the roller. *They did not have the pulley*, so that the blocks could not be hauled up and gently lowered into place. That no pulleys have been found does not, in itself, prove that they did not exist. But other facts lead to this conclusion. For instance, in the many representations of Ancient Egyptian ships there are no pulleys at the mast-head. The yards had to be *pushed* up; and in some tomb-paintings sailors are shown doing this. Again, if pulleys had been used, tongs or "lewises" would have been needed to grab the blocks, and would have left marks. No such marks have been found.

The method of construction seems to have been as follows. First, the foundations were levelled by "running a watercourse along and about the surface to be levelled, and then measuring down from the surface at many points simultaneously, thus establishing datum points to which the complete surface would be eventually reduced" (Engelbach). This would explain the slight error which exists in the level of the platform which runs partly under the Great Pyramid. It is on a perfect plane, but slopes up about 6 inches from the north-east to the south-east corner. If when the points were being checked a north-east wind had been blowing, this would have produced the error.

The stones were dragged on wooden sleds up the causeway leading to the pyramid, and the first course laid on the virgin rock. When the top had been levelled the workmen were ready for the next course. They built a ramp leading up to the top of the first course, and up this they dragged the blocks, levering them into position. While that course was being laid, the ramp would be built up and extended, getting longer and longer with each course, since the angle of incline would have to remain the same. Engelbach believes that the reason for the thin layer of mortar between the blocks was not to hold them in position (their weight alone would have been sufficient) but because there was no other way in which a block weighing several tons could have been pushed "home" against its neighbour, "unless it were, so to speak, floating on a thin bed of wet, viscid mortar. I believe that this is the explanation of the mortar and the almost perfect smoothness of the tops."

Similar methods must have been used in building the temples with their pillars and pylons. It was a matter of careful planning, a few simple mechanical aids, and the organisation of abundant man-power.

The Egyptians were greatly helped in their building operations by river transport. They rarely had to carry heavy loads great distances overland, since the country bordered the river along its entire length. Boats, as we have seen, played a vital part, and vessels of quite large size were built even in the pre-Dynastic period (before 3200 B.C.) Even in the time of Snofru (Third Dynasty) there is a record of a boat of 100 cubits (172 feet), and by the Eighteenth Dynasty they were carrying loads of more than 650 tons. These vessels were of many types: warships, cattle-boats, freighters, and private yachts. . . . There are many representations of boat-builders, whose craft must have been in continual demand.

However, they were handicapped in the early stages by a lack of suitable timber, since broad planks were unobtainable from such native Egyptian trees as the sycamore fig; therefore the Egyptian boat-builders developed a special method of construction, utilising small planks, which Herodotus saw and described:

". . . They cut a quantity of planks about 2 cubits (41 inches) in length, arranging the planks like bricks, and attaching them by ties to a number of long stakes or poles till the hull is complete. They give the boat no ribs, but caulk the seams with papyrus from inside."

A series of thwarts prevented the boat from collapsing outward, while stout cables attached at each end and passing over fixed stays in the side of the hull maintained rigidity lengthwise. In boats such as these the Egyptians made long journeys and carried great loads. But one should beware of being misled by Ancient Egyptian artists who show 500-ton obelisks lashed to the *decks* of large boats, which would obviously be top-heavy. Most probably these big loads were carried on rafts.

Carpentry, at which the Egyptians were adept, may have developed out of boat-building. Complete mastery over wood had been achieved by the time of the First Dynasty, as we know from the elaborately carved and inlaid cabinets which have survived. The native woods were sycamore, willow, tamarisk, *persea* and *sidder* (Arabic, *nabq*). Cedar and cypress were imported before 3000 B.C., and later they used ebony, fir, yew, and beech. Nearly all the joints used by carpenters to-day were known 5,000 years ago. Third Dynasty coffins exist with halved, mitred, and concealed mitre joints. During the same period (2800 B.C.) the Egyptians were making plywood consisting of six different layers of different woods. Nails were usually wooden pegs, but tiny gold nails were used for affixing veneers. Tenon and mortise joints were also known at this early period, and were much used for the joining of the narrow planks which were all that could be obtained from native timber. The chariots are fine examples of the carpenter's art, light and strong, with double spokes.

Practically the only modern carpenter's tool which the Ancient Egyptian did not possess was the plane, but he could do such fine work with the adze that he did not need it. Many examples of these tools have been preserved in Egyptian tombs; squares, levels, chisels, mallets, saws which differ very little from their modern counterparts.[1]

And yet by the learned scribes of Ancient Egypt

[1] See illustration opposite p. 160.

these brilliant craftsmen were held in low esteem. A poet of the Middle Empire writes of the metal-worker:

> "I have never seen the smith as an ambassador,
>   or the goldsmith carry tidings;
> Yet I have seen the smith at his work
> At the mouth of his furnace,
> His fingers were like crocodile [hide]
> He stank more than the roe of fish. . . ."

And of the woodcarver the same scribe writes:

> "Each artist who works with the chisel
> Tires himself more than he who hoes [a field]
> The wood is his field, of metal are his tools.
>   In the night—is he free?
> He works more than his arms are able,
> In the night—he lights a light."[1]

The men and women who wove the clothes which the Egyptians wore are unsung, yet throughout the long span of Egyptian civilisation theirs was a highly important craft employing hundreds of thousands. Erman says:

". . . They lavished all their skill in the one endeavour to prepare the finest and whitest linen that was possible, and they certainly brought their linen to great perfection; I need only remind my readers of the white garments worn by men of rank, which were so fine that their limbs could be seen gleaming through them. Some of this very fine linen that we possess is almost comparable to our silken materials for smoothness and softness."

Cotton, of course, was unknown, so that the weaving industry consisted entirely in the weaving of linen. They cultivated flax from very early times, boiling it in a large vessel which is represented in Middle Kingdom tomb-paintings. The idea was to free the outer covering of the stalks, and afterwards they were beaten with hammers

[1] In our own age the scribe is more likely to burn the midnight oil than the artisan.—L.C.

until the outside was loosened or destroyed. The flax which was thus obtained had then to be cleaned and separated from the rubbish before it could be used. In the Middle Kingdom this process was carried out by hand: men are shown carefully picking out the good fibres and laying them together to form a thread. But in the time of Rekhmire the weavers used a comb, as is done to-day.

There are some interesting examples of weavers' looms and shuttles in the British Museum which show that in principle the method was basically the same as that used to-day, but, of course, everything was done by hand. The thread was moistened, and then twisted together with a spindle. Close by on the ground stood a pot containing the rough threads; the person spinning allowed the thread to run over his or her hand or over a fork. Great skill was shown. In one picture we see women managing two spindles at the same time, and twisting each of the two threads from two different kinds of flax. They managed to do this by balancing themselves on a stool, first removing practically every stitch of clothing, so that the two spindles and the threads should not get entangled in their dresses.

The Egyptians were also highly skilled in the treatment of animal skins. Beautiful skins, especially those which were spotted or patterned, were used in the manufacture of seat-coverings, shields, and quivers. Panther-skins seem to have been especially valued.

However, only the rich could afford the fine linen garments. The poor would have to be content with the coarsest material or the hides of animals.

Other arts in which the Egyptians excelled were rope-making (necessary for the hauling of huge monuments), faience and glass-making. Specimens exist of rope made from palm fibre 5 inches thick. These ropes are as strong and well-made as any made to-day. Faience reached a very high standard; it was made from finely-powdered quartz mixed with an adhesive (probably natron) and then fired. The

Egyptians used it for vases and making statuettes, such as the well-known *shawabti* figures which are found in hundreds in the tombs. They also made glass objects, but glass-blowing did not come into use until Roman times. The Egyptian method was to wind drawn rods of glass round a cone, then reheat, roll and polish. Or it could be cast, as in the case of the beautiful glass head-rest found in Tutankhamun's tomb. Gold was mined in enormous quantities in Nubia and elsewhere, and the art of the Egyptian goldsmith at its best approaches the finest work of the Italian Renaissance. Gold was used for plating an immense variety of objects, and such a vast quantity was available that Tushratta, King of Mittani, could write to Amenophis IV (Akhnaten):

"Send me much gold, more gold, for in my brother's [i.e. Akhnaten's] land gold is as common as dust. . . ."

The solid gold coffin of Tutankhamun, one of the greatest masterpieces of Ancient Egyptian art, weighs 300 lb. avoirdupois. In the time of Sheshonq of the Twentieth Dynasty the weight of gold and silver given to the Temple amounted to more than 20 tons.

These lovely things pay perpetual tribute to the skill of the Egyptian craftsmen. We can marvel at the magnificent gold mask of Tutankhamun; we shall never know who made it.[1] The thousands who toiled on the Pyramids, who raised the drum-columns in the Hypostyle Hall at Karnak, who fashioned the alabaster vases, the inlaid ebony and ivory caskets, the necklaces of carnelian and lapis-lazuli, have only these things as their memorial. Only occasionally an archaeologist finds in a rubbish-tip near the Pyramids a scrap of rope, a workman's basket, or few copper tools, mute witnesses of the anonymous millions who laboured for the few.

[1] See illustration opposite p. 161.

CHAPTER XI

MAGIC AND MEDICINE

SEVERAL months have passed, and again we are in the great house of the Vizier Rekhmire. But the atmosphere is now very different from that which we remember from our last visit. There is no sound of music from the women's quarters; the servants go about their tasks quietly, and no-one sings. When we meet Rekhmire walking across the courtyard with his wife they look grave. For Nofret, the Vizier's eldest daughter, has been stricken down with a fever.

Let us follow the parents as they enter their daughter's bedchamber. Several other members of the family are there; Ta-kha'et with her husband Sinuhe (for since we last met them they have been married), and the eldest son, Menkheperre-Sonb, and his wife. They stand a little apart from the bed on which Nofret lies. Her face is flushed and shiny with sweat; she puts her hand to her brow and moans; every now and again her slim body is convulsed with a rigor, and she says, "I am cold. . . . I am cold. . . ."

Near her stands the Court Physician with his assistants. But he is not looking at Nofret. He is leaning over a small table on which stands a magical amulet, a knotted cord, and small jars containing drugs. He makes magical passes over the amulet and the cord, rapidly repeating a spell, while one of his assistants makes responses. After a while he takes the amulet and fastens it to the girl's dress, above her heart. Then he ties the cord loosely around her forehead. After more movements of his hands above the body of his patient, he moves across the room to the waiting relatives.

Together they leave the room, leaving only a serving-woman to watch over the sick girl.

"Within a day and a night, if Amun is merciful," he says, "the demon will have left her. . . ."

.   .   .   .

Five hundred miles away, in a desert valley near the Orontes, Senmut, the officer of charioteers, lies unconscious in a tent. A few hours ago, while commanding the rear-guard, he had run into an ambush in a narrow defile. The Bedouins had rolled rocks down on to the track, blocking the way, then poured down on the Pharaoh's army while they were still in column of route. Unable to manœuvre, the charioteers had had to dismount and fight it out hand to hand. It had been a desperate struggle in which young Kenamun had distinguished himself by his courage and intelligence.

Early in the fight the enemy had noted Senmut, whose rank was easily distinguished by his dress and by his standard-bearer, and had marked him out for special attack. Both he and his charioteer were wounded by the first flight of arrows; the horses were killed and the chariot overturned. Half-blinded by blood, Senmut had found himself surrounded by Bedouin spearmen. He had killed two before a third brought him down with a mace-blow to the side of the helmet. Senmut fell just as Kenamun, who had seen his plight, fought his way through to him with a band of spearmen and drove off the Bedouin. But before doing this he had sent a few bold warriors, including trumpeters, to fight their way out of the ambush and warn the main body of the army. A few had got through; Tuthmosis heard the trumpets far off along the valley and had sent infantry to the rescue. The Bedouins had been driven off into the hills after heavy slaughter, leaving a hundred dead and dying. Then Kenamun brought his friend's unconscious body to the tent of the Chief Physician. He is standing by now, an anxious look on his bandaged face as he watches the great man performing an operation by the light of oil lamps.

There is no magic here. First the physician cleans out the arrow wounds, staunches the flow of blood and neatly stitches the severed flesh. He makes a careful examination and finds that Senmut's left arm and leg are paralysed. He examines the abrasion on the skull, ascertains that there is no fracture, but recognises that the paralysis is due to pressure on the brain which must be relieved.

His surgical instruments lie on a table beside the bed: curved knives of various shapes, drills, and saws. With a small sharp saw, he removes a portion of the skull and cuts away the membrane so that the brain lies exposed. Delicately removing the clotted blood and cleaning the damaged tissues, he stitches the membrane back in place, replaces the piece of skull, and binds it in position with bandages and adhesive.

It is already dawn when he rises to his feet; the neighing of horses and the distant braying of trumpets come faintly across the still air. In answer to Kenamun's unspoken question, the doctor says:

"I cannot say. It is too early to tell."

He places his hand on Senmut's chest.

"His heart is good. He may survive. But he cannot be moved for a long time. He must stay here for some weeks; then perhaps he can be moved to Kadesh."

Smiling at Kenamun's anxious face, he drops his hand on the young man's shoulder and remarks:

"Don't worry, my son. Like all you soldiers, he has a very thick skull. . . ."

*　　　*　　　*

Fanciful? Not at all. Such operations were performed by the Ancient Egyptians, even in pre-Dynastic times, and a number of skulls have been found which bear evidence of trepanning; and the patient sometimes survived, as is proved by the fact that the severed section of the skull had knit to the parent bone. Other operations as delicate as this were performed by Egyptian surgeons, as we know from the Edwin Smith Surgical Papyrus, which dates from the beginning of the New Kingdom (*c.* 1500 B.C.) This, the oldest book of surgery in the world, contains a total of forty-eight cases, ranging from injuries of the cranium to the lower spine, methodically arranged.

Writing of this magnificent manuscript, Dr. P. G. Sobhy Bey, Emeritus Professor of Medicine and History of Medicine, Fouad I University, says:

"Each case is preceded by a brief caption expressing a summary diagnosis, followed by another detailed diagnosis, a brief but clearly formulated prognosis and sometimes the therapy. In most cases a later [Egyptian] commentator added one or more explanatory notes [glosses] to the original text in order to interpret expressions difficult to understand, or to expound obscure passages containing words or expressions which have become obsolete since the original text of the manuscript."

This papyrus must therefore have been one of the standard text-books used in the Egyptian medical schools, and was certainly much older than the date of the present manuscript. In fact, it may be 5,000 years old.

There are other medical papyri, such as the Ebers Papyrus, which deals with boils, cysts, and the like, and the Kahûn Papyrus, which is concerned with gynaecological cases. There is also the Chester-Beatty Papyrus, part of which gives prescriptions and remedies for affections of the anus and rectum, and the Hearst Papyrus, which contains 250 prescriptions or sections. Other papyri are present in the British Museum and in Turin. Some of these papyri contain almost identical sections and seem to have been transcribed from one master work.

What can we learn from them concerning the Egyptians'

knowledge of the human body? First, that they had a better knowledge of anatomy than other ancient peoples, due almost certainly to the custom of embalmment and mummification. Warren R. Dawson, in *The Legacy of Egypt*, writes:

"The custom provided for the first time opportunities for observations in comparative anatomy, for it enabled its practitioners to recognise the analogies between the viscera of the human body and those of animals, the latter long familiar from the time-honoured custom of cutting up animals for food and for sacrifice. It is a noteworthy fact that the various hieroglyphic signs representing parts of the body, and especially the internal organs, are pictures of the organs of mammals and not of human beings. This shows that the Egyptians' knowledge of mammalian anatomy was older than their knowledge of that of man, and, further, that they recognised the essential identity of the two by devising signs based on the organs of animals and using them unaltered when referring to the corresponding organs in the human body."

In the ancient language there are no less than 200 anatomical terms, proving that the Ancient Egyptians could recognise and differentiate between a wide variety of human organs which a less enlightened people would have lumped together. But there were many blanks in their knowledge. They recognised the importance of the heart:

"The beginning of the science of the physician; to know the movement of the heart; there are vessels attached to it for every movement of the body. . . ."

But they did not perceive the circulation of the blood. They had one word to denote muscles, arteries, and veins. The word used for blood-vessels communicating with the heart is the same as that used for the muscles. They also thought that the heart was the seat of the intelligence and the emotions, and attached little importance to the brain—except that they had observed that damage to the brain affected certain muscles of the body. So important was the heart considered that the embalmers always replaced it in the body before burial, though they removed the other organs for separate embalmment. However, as Warren Dawson says—

". . . there remained a nucleus of correctly observed truth which suggests that in very early times a serious attempt was being made to understand the structure and functions of the body and its organs, and the effects of injuries on them. It was observed, for instance (as we learn from the Edwin Smith Papyrus) that the brain is enclosed in a membrane and that its hemispheres are patterned with convolutions; that injury to the brain causes a loss of control over various parts of the body, the tension of the facial muscles and other manifestations . . . that certain injuries can be confidently cured, and others, again, are definitely hopeless."

It may be asked why the Egyptians, who used skilled surgery for the treatment of wounds, resorted to magic when faced with internal disorders which had no obvious cause? Why should Nofret's malaria be treated magically and Senmut's concussion rationally? And remember that there was no clear distinction between magician and physician. They were one and the same. If Senmut had developed malaria, the physician would have applied the same treatment to him as his colleague in Thebes applied to Nofret.

The answer seems to be that where there was no obvious cause for an illness it was attributed to the presence of evil spirits within the body of the patient. The physician's task then was to drive the demon out, either by conjuration, exorcism, or the application of drugs which were originally chosen for their magical rather than their therapeutic properties. Medicine, in fact, developed out of magic, and he would be a bold man who affirmed that magic has entirely disappeared from medical practice, even to-day. Only nowadays we call it "having faith in the doctor".

Thus in Egyptian papyri, such as the Ebers and the Hearst, the doctor harangues the demon within the patient's body, or implies that the suffering is due to some poison emanating from the demon which has lodged in the body of the sufferer. If spells were found ineffective, the next recourse was to concoctions of so repellent a nature as to force the offending spirit to quit. People who complain of having to take unpleasant-tasting medicine may be thankful that they did not live in Ancient Egypt, they might have been expected to swallow crushed (or live) insects, excreta, or various revolting forms of animal or vegetable life. Incidentally, these Ancient Egyptian prescriptions, passing to Europe via Greek, Roman, or Arab medical text-books, reappeared in the magical formulae of witches in medieval and later periods; indeed, they survive even to-day as folk-superstitions. The incantation of Macbeth's Weird Sisters might almost have come from an Egyptian doctor's book of prescriptions:

> ". . . Eye of newt and toe of frog,
> Wool of bat and tongue of dog
> Adder's fork and blind-worm's sting,
> Lizard's leg and howlet's wing . . .
> Scale of dragon, tooth of wolf,
> Witches' mummy. . . ."

and so on.

Sir Alan Gardiner, writing of the Egyptian magician's art, has defined two parts of his performance, the *oral rite* and the *manual rite*. In certain of the medical papyri ("medico-magical" would be a better word) there are often directions for the performance of the manual rite (i.e. a ritual) to accompany the preceding oral rite.

"The manual rite often took the form of reciting the words over an image of clay, a string of beads, a knotted cord, a piece of inscribed linen . . . or some other object. These objects, thus magically charged, were generally placed upon or attached to the patient's body."

Alternative prescriptions were given if the first failed.

What kind of diseases did the Ancient Egyptians suffer from? We can learn quite a lot from statuary, paintings, and from the examination of mummies. Doctors have identified cases of infantile paralysis, Pott's disease, and rickets. Eye diseases—trachoma and ophthalmia—were common, as they are in modern Egypt. Bilharziasis, the terrible debilitating disease from which more than 80 per cent. of the peasant population suffers to-day—and which is carried by certain species of snails which breed in the irrigation canals—was known in ancient times, and the bilharzia worm has been found in mummies.

The Ancient Egyptians had dental troubles, and were treated by skilled dental surgeons:

"In a tomb of the pyramid period a skull was found showing clear evidence of a successful operation for the drainage of an abscess at the root of the first molar. Another skull showed two teeth skilfully tied together with gold wire, evidently to fasten a loose tooth to its more stable neighbour and so to prevent it falling out. . . ." (Dr. Sobhy Bey).

There were also eye doctors, bowel specialists—"Guardians of the Anus"—and physicians who specialised in internal diseases "who know the secret and specialise in the body fluids". The medical papyri contain prescriptions for treating diseases of the lungs, liver, stomach, bladder, and for various affections of the head and scalp (including recipes for preventing the hair falling out or turning grey). There are prescriptions for rheumatic and arthritic complaints and for women's diseases.

Many of these remedies and prescriptions have been passed on to us via the writings of Pliny, Dioscorides, Galen, and other Greek writers.

"The works of the classical writers," says Dawson, "are . . . often merely the stepping-stones by which much of the ancient medical lore reached Europe, apart from direct borrowings. . . .

From Egypt we have the earliest medical books, the first observations in anatomy, the first experiments in surgery and pharmacy, the first use of splints, bandages, compresses, and other appliances, and the first anatomical and medical vocabulary. . . ."

So beware of despising the Ancient Egyptians because their doctors began by using magic. Many of the drugs they prescribed had genuine therapeutic value, and indeed are still used in modern pharmacy. For example; acacia, anise, barley, cassia, castor beans, castor oil, wormwood, coriander, cucumber, cumin, poppy, saffron are among the vegetable substances; among the mineral, alum, copper, feldspar, sulphur, red ochre, sodium carbonate and bicarbonate, arsenic and nitre (the name is Egyptian) have been identified in the medical papyri. And among the animal substances used were the fats of animals, blood, bone marrow, bile, liver, and spleen.

Clearly, over thousands of years, those substances which had proved most successful in the treatment of particular diseases would always be prescribed for those diseases; thus scientific medicine grew by degrees out of magic. Dr. Sobhy Bey, to whom I am indebted for some of the material in this chapter, disagrees strongly with those who dismiss most of Egyptian pharmacy as magical "hit-or-miss" therapy and little more. Dr. Sobhy, who has the advantage of being both a distinguished physician and a student of Egyptology, writes:

". . . The various prescriptions (in the Ebers and Hearst Papyri) seem to be quite rational and natural applications to the alleviation of symptoms—complexes of knowledge of general physiological properties and actions of plant, animal and mineral medica. Notice, for example, the drugs cited to kill intestinal worms and those to purge or stop diarrhoeas . . . the very small magical parts of the papyri ought not to be exaggerated."

When I last met Dr. Sobhy in Cairo he told me a story which I have reason to believe, since he has studied Ancient

Egyptian medicine for many years; however, I have not had the opportunity of checking it from any other source. It is that in one of the medical papyri there is a prescription for the treatment of wounds or open sores. The ancient physician prescribes a certain type of *fungus* which grows on still water.

Penicillin in 2000 B.C.? Too fanciful, perhaps. But one never knows.

CHAPTER XII

BUYING AND SELLING

IT is afternoon. Two figures are moving down the long, dusty, crowded road to the dockside of Thebes. One is a tall, broad-shouldered Nubian, who holds firmly the hand of a small, excited boy. The lad points eagerly to right and left. He drags at his companion's arm, urging him to stay. Here is a man with a performing monkey; there a young girl dancing, surrounded by a circle of hand-clapping men who squat in the dust. Nearby a female contortionist gravely ties her supple limbs into knots. There are so many things to distract a small boy; but his tall companion walks resolutely on, looking neither to right or left. He dare not; for the small boy is Per-hor, son of the Vizier, and his companion is only the porter who keeps guard at the door of the great man's house. A trusted servant, he has been instructed to meet Per-hor at the school gate and escort him home, but the youngster has persuaded the Nubian to let him see the market.

When they arrive at the quays, two great ships which have brought corn from the north are being unloaded. The corn is intended for the treasury of Amun, and scribes sit vigilantly watching the unloading, and noting down the number of sacks as they are brought ashore on the backs of the sweating porters. But not all the corn is going to its official destination. The crews of the ships have each received a measure of corn as part of their wages and some are already haggling with the merchants who sit cross-legged on the quay with their jars and baskets. No coin is exchanged, for none exists. All trading is by barter.

Per-hor drags his guardian through the crowd, darting first to this side and then to that. Here is a fish-dealer squatting before his rush basket. A woman tries to beat down the price. Nearby another tradesman has ointment to sell. Another offers small white cakes. A man offers a collar in exchange, but the cake-seller refuses with a scornful wave of the hand. "Then take these sandals as well,"[1] says the prospective buyer, and the deal is done.

Here sits another dealer with a basket of red and blue ornaments. Next to him another man is selling fish-hooks. Brown-skinned sailors look down from the decks; one of them tosses a bunch of dates to a group of giggling girls.

*   *   *

Not one person in this great crowd of buyers and sellers receives cash wage or salary. All payments and transactions are in kind. The same system applies to the very top of the social scale. The great officials derive their wealth from the estates which they own or administer on behalf of the King, who is the greatest landowner. To us, with our elaborate banking and currency systems, such an arrangement seems primitive, yet the Ancient Egyptians did not find it inconvenient. They held markets, paid salaries, lent on interest and collected taxes without a coin changing hands. On the other hand, although a man might exchange geese for corn, cattle for timber, the relative value of the goods would be assessed in terms of some common object of known value.

Under the New Empire one of the measures of value was a spiral of copper wire, called the *uten*. This measure became so firmly established that a spiral became the hieroglyphic sign for the *uten*. This does not mean that these copper spirals changed hands in the market, except perhaps to adjust some slight difference in value, but the value

[1] This scene is from a tomb at Sakkarah.

of objects of the most diverse kinds were related to them.

The servant Thothmes of the Temple of Thoth was presented with a bill by the tax authorities in which the value of each object was assessed in this way. Here is part of the assessment:

"Skin, raw, 4 pieces, worth in copper 8 *uten*.

"Skins, made up into coats of mail, 1 piece, worth in copper 5 *uten*.

"Stick, prop-stick, inlaid work, 1 piece, worth in copper, 4 *uten*.

"Hoe, worth in copper 2 *uten*", etc., etc.

Erman, in his *Life in Ancient Egypt*, mentions another transaction in which 119 *uten* of copper were paid for an ox—

"but of these 119 *uten* not one metal *uten* changed hands. A stick with inlaid work was substituted for 25 *uten*, another of less elaborate design for 12 *uten*, 11 jars of honey for 11 *uten*, and so on."

Another Egyptian unit was the *deben*, a word originally meaning "ring"; but after a time it appears to have come to signify not the object itself, but its weight or value. Similar units of value existed in other civilisations; the Chaldeans at one time seem to have used bars of metal, and among African and other primitive tribes to-day beads and other objects of convenient size are used in similar fashion.

Internal trade within Egypt seems to have been on a relatively small scale. The reason is simple. Each *nome*, or province, was self-supporting, producing everything needed by its inhabitants. Each royal or priestly estate had its weavers, its brewers, its carpenters and other craftsmen, and the peasants themselves grew the food which they ate. There can be no comparison with the complex industrial

civilisations of our own day, when a housewife can enter a
shop and buy products which come from all over the world.
There was no need for merchants as we understand the
name; unlike the later Phoenicians and the Greeks, who
were carriers and middlemen, the Egyptians supplied their
own needs.

The only exception to this rule was in the field of foreign
trade. At various times Egypt had a lively commerce with
neighbouring countries, sometimes, as in the case of Nubia,
Syria, and Libya, with lands which had come under their
control, but at other times with lands, such as the Aegean
islands and "The land of Punt" (Somaliland), which were
too remote for conquest.

Nubia (the modern Sudan) was known to the Egyptians
as far back as the Old Kingdom and possibly earlier; from
time to time inroads were made into the country and its
people forced to pay tribute. The kings of the Twelfth
Dynasty were particularly active in this area, and one of the
commonest representations in royal and other monuments
is a line of Negro prisoners, their hands manacled, the
women with children on their backs. From Nubia, either
by trade or conquest, came ivory, ebony, gold, and precious
stones, and such exotic imports as ostrich feathers (for fans),
ostrich eggs, monkeys, panthers and giraffes.

These were mainly loot which went to swell the treasuries
of Pharaoh and the Amun priesthood. But with other
countries the Egyptians undoubtedly carried on trade.
There was, for instance, the mysterious "land of Punt" of
which the whereabouts are uncertain; some writers have
suggested that it may have lain on the west coast of India,
but the generally accepted opinion is that it lay on the
African coast to the south of the Red Sea, in the area
occupied by modern Somaliland.

In the great empire built by Queen Hapshepsut (the
predecessor of Tuthmosis III) at Deir-el-Bahir is a famous
sculptured relief depicting in fascinating detail an expedition

to Punt carried out under the Queen's direction. Much of
it survives to-day just as it appeared to little Per-hor and
Kenamun, his brother, and generations of young men in
whom it must have stirred the lust for travel.

Erman's description of this relief cannot be bettered:

"In one of the harbours of the Red Sea lies the fleet, which the
soldiers of Her Majesty are to conduct to that distant country;
the stately vessels are about 65 feet in length, and they are
provided with thirty rowers and with gigantic sails, which stand
out like wings beyond both sides of the ship. The great jars which
contain the provisions are being conveyed on board by a rowing
boat; on the shore, however, near the trees to which the ships are
tied, a sacrifice is being offered to the goddess 'Hathor, Lady of
Punt' that 'she may send wind'. Then the sails are hoisted up, the
sailors climb the yards to make fast the last ropes, the rowers dip
their long oars in the water, and from the wooden partitions
in the bows, in which the two captains stand, resounds the
command, 'To larboard.' The ships begin to move, and thus
'the royal soldiers voyage on the sea, they begin their
beautiful journey to the Divine Land, and voyage happily to
Punt'."

Further along the wall another relief shows the arrival
at Punt. The artist, who may have made the voyage himself, has depicted primitive huts built on piles, each with a
ladder leading to a single door. These miserable dwellings,
set among luxuriant tropical vegetation, aroused the con-
tempt of the civilised Egyptians. The men wear skirts and
have pointed beards and pigtails, just as they are represented
in the reliefs of the time of Khufu, more than 1,000 years
earlier. As the Egyptians disembark, the men of Punt
advance with suitable humility, led by their chief, whose
huge wife suffers from elephantiasis. Her grotesque figure
provides a butt for the cruel wit of the artist. The unfortunate woman, described satirically as "the princess",
bulges out of her shapeless clothing, and behind her is an

ass, under which an inscription reads: "The donkey which carries his wife."

Then trading commences. Up and down the gangplanks hurry the Egyptians, carrying ebony, ivory, "white gold from the country of Amu, sweet-scented woods, all manner of eye-pigments, baboons, monkeys and greyhounds, slaves and their children. Never has the like been brought to any king whatsoever since the beginning of time."

But the most important product of Punt is the incense for which the country is famous. Not only do the Egyptians carry back piles of incense, but numbers of growing incense trees are carried aboard, to be replanted in Egypt.

And what do the people of Punt get in exchange? On a table set up on the beach the delighted natives examine the goods which the foreigners have brought; gay necklets, daggers and battle-axes, besides bread, beer, wine, fruits "and all good things of Egypt"—all, one suspects, of considerably lower value than the products for which they are being exchanged.

The Egyptians, as we have seen, also had commerce with Crete and the "Isles of the Great Sea", and with Syria. Egyptian weapon-makers travelled in the land of Retenu, selling their wares, and Semitic girls were often bought or taken as slaves.

Some of the objects imported into Egypt from Syria and bartered for corn and other products, were ships, chariots, carriages, weapons, musical instruments, drinks ("the beer of Quede, the wine of Charu"), horses, bulls, cows, and other cattle.

But hardly any of this wealth reached the mass of the people. Most of it went into the store-rooms of the King and the Treasuries of the Gods. Having no means with which to buy food, the Egyptian workmen were dependent entirely on the will of their masters for mere sustenance.

All, from the highest to the lowest, were ruthlessly taxed,
and one might ask how, since the Egyptians had no mone-
tary system, were these taxes gathered? With the peasants
and the farmers, it was relatively simple: they gave up a
portion of the produce of their land, their crops and cattle
and the cloth which was woven and spun by their wives
and daughters. But how were the numerous scribes and
officials assessed and taxed?

These men owed their power and wealth to gifts be-
stowed by the King, i.e. by the State. In return for his
services, a high official might receive, as a mark of esteem
and honour, a beautiful villa, a fine carriage, a splendid
boat, numerous Negro and other slaves, beside cattle, food,
wine, and clothing. The snag, from the official's point of
view, was that all these gifts were *registered in his name*.
When the tax-gatherers made their assessment, they could
estimate to a fair degree the extent and nature of the man's
wealth, and taxed him accordingly.

The Ancient Egyptians, of all degrees of society, paid
their taxes with no better grace than we do to-day, and
there survive in documents numerous complaints of unfair
assessment, extortion, and injustice.

Here is one, from a shepherd of the name of Thothmes,
who had lost a donkey, on whose work he was to be taxed.
Apparently, one Paere, who should have given it up, had
kept the animal:

"Channa, the officer of the company *Shining as the Sun* stationed
in the country of D'aper, gave you a donkey and told you to give
it to Thothmes. But you have not given it to me. Then I seized
you when you were in Memphis with Amenmose the chief of the
stable, and said to you, 'Give it to me.' You then said to me,
'Don't take me to court; I have the donkey, but if you send to
fetch it I will give it up.' So you said, and you swore by the life of
your lord that you would cause it to be brought to me. Behold,
however, you have *not* sent it to me, and now they[1] demand from

[1] The tax-collectors.

me the work of the donkey, year by year, while it has been with you."[1]

It appears, therefore, that we have little reason to envy the Ancient Egyptians, except for the fact that they had no income tax forms to fill up!

[1] Erman, *Everyday Life in Ancient Egypt*.

CHAPTER XIV

HOUSE OF ETERNITY

AUTUMN has come, and with it the Inundation. Far, far to the south, the waters of the Blue Nile, swollen by rains, are rushing into the main stream, bearing a rich treasure of fertilising mud from the mountains of Abyssinia. But the Ancient Egyptians have never heard of Abyssinia, or the Blue Nile. For them the world ends south of Nubia, and the life-giving flood, the yearly miracle, comes as the gift of Re. At Thebes and other towns along the serpentine length of the river, the priests are studying the "Nilometers", measuring the level of the flood-water and comparing it with those of previous years. It is a "good Nile" this year, and already scribes are calculating the expected yield of the land, and the amount of taxation which can be levied. The river began to rise three months ago, in August, when the Egyptians held the High Nile Festival. Last month, September, it was at its highest. Now it is October, and in a few weeks it will begin to subside, and sowing will commence in November.

A strange stillness broods over the imperial city. Where, a few months ago, there were green fields stretching to the foot of the limestone hills there is now a lake-like expanse of water. You can take a boat from the quayside on the eastern bank and land within a short distance of the Necropolis on the western side. Many of the peasants are idle, but some have been recruited for work on the monuments. Big boats are arriving from distant Assuan loaded with granite, and in the Temple of Karnak work is being done on the reconstruction and extension of the Temple. Gangs of sweating men haul on ropes, grunting a rhythmic to enable the King and his train to enter the Temple.

Outside, beyond the first pylon with its fluttering pennons, a broad avenue of sphinxes stretches in a straight line to the quayside. Stand on that quay and look to right and left along the river bank and you will see lines of troops —brown-skinned Egyptians with their spears and shields, coal-black Negroes from the Sudan, and foreign auxiliaries, such as the Shardana, wearing horned helmets. And behind them, talking, gesticulating, struggling to see over the backs of the soldiers, are thousands of common people. Every yard of the route along which the King will pass is thick with them.

Suddenly a mighty shout goes up. Far out across the sunlit river a great flotilla of boats is approaching: the royal barge, golden in the sun, the barges carrying the court officials, the royal bodyguard, and the river police. Menkheperre, the mighty conqueror, the scourge of Egypt's enemies, is once again coming to offer sacrifice to his father, Amun, and bringing rich spoils of war to enrich the Temple of the King of Gods. This is the forty-second year of his reign. Seventeen times during those forty-two years he has led his armies out of Thebes, and seventeen times he has returned victorious. From Nubia in the south to the far-off Euphrates in the east, scores of petty kingdoms owe allegiance to Pharaoh, and the kings of the neighbouring states, of Mittani and of Hittites, stand in fear of him.

> "I myself have stretched out my two hands,
> I have bound them for thee. . . ."

So Amun is made to address Tuthmosis in a hymn of victory:

"The earth in its length and breadth, Westerners and Easterners, are subject to thee.
Thou tramplest all countries, thy heart glad;
None presents himself before thy majesty,

While I am thy leader, so that thou mayest reach them,
Thou hast crossed the water of the Great Bend[1] of Naharin, with
victory, with might. . . ."

In the inner courtyard the great officials cease whispering
and stand in nervous silence. Rekhmire fiddles with a gold
armlet; the General Amenemhab adjusts his helmet;
Nofret pushes back the curls of her wig. There is a distant
shrilling of trumpets and the roar of the crowd is louder,
so that now their cry can be heard:

"Life! Prosperity! Health! . . . Life! Prosperity! Health!"

The ranks of shaven priests look towards the great
bronze gates, which stand open. They hear the tramp of
feet, the sound of hooves, the rumble of chariot wheels.
The procession is entering the outer courtyard, where
thousands prostrate themselves, their foreheads in the dust.

"Life! Prosperity! Health! . . . Life! Prosperity! Health!"
shout a thousand voices.

Shadows fall across the bronze doors. The cavalcade is
entering. First, ranks of priests in white robes, then officers
of the Royal Bodyguard, marching slowly, their young
faces set and unsmiling under their high, plumed head-
dresses, gold gleaming on their bare arms, their spear-tips
catching the sun; then the fan-bearers holding huge
ostrich-feather fans; and now, born aloft in a golden
palanquin on the shoulders of twelve noblemen, the
Pharaoh himself. With one movement, all except the priests
and highest officials prostrate themselves.

The slim priestesses, led by Nofret, advance slowly,
shaking their *systra*, and singing:

"How splendid is he who returns in victory!
For Amun hath caused him to smite the princes of Palestine."

[1] The Euphrates.

And the deep-voiced priests reply:

> "All folk, all folk of the House of Amun are in festival,
> For Amun-Re loveth the Ruler. . . ."

Tuthmosis III is a small man with a plump, unmilitary face. He is over seventy, but years of arduous campaigning have toughened his frame and hardened his features. His bare, sunburned arms are muscular, and his carriage is that of a younger man. He wears the tall double crown which has symbolised for 1,500 years the union of the Two Lands. On his brow are the twin insignia of Upper and Lower Egypt, the falcon and the serpent. And in each strong hand he carries another symbol—the crook, representing Upper Egypt, and the flail for lower Egypt. He wears a long skirt of gauffered linen, and he is shod with golden sandals.[1]

*　　　　*　　　　*

If we could be miraculously transported back to that time, if we could stand unseen, among the prostrate, adoring crowd—

> "among them, but not of them; in a shroud
> Of thoughts which were not their thoughts"

we would probably feel amused or indignant. Some of us would see only a pathetic little human being, in a hat too big for him, surrounded by ridiculous pomp, the creature of a corrupt court and a cynical priesthood who exploited the superstitions of the masses for their own selfish ends, That would be the Marxist analysis. And even the more tolerant among us would feel a sentimental pity for the toiling millions who built his monuments, laboured in his fields and shed their blood in his wars. "The Pharaoh's people," we would think. . . . "Poor devils."

But we would be wrong. That was not how the Ancient Egyptians felt about their king, and if we are to enter into

[1] See illustration opposite p. 176.

their minds we shall have to make a considerable effort of
the imagination.

In the first place, his function was fundamentally
religious. He was a priest-king. He was the intermediary
between the people and the unseen powers which controlled
the fate of men. He was also the people's representative in
a far more profound sense than that implied by the modern
use of the phrase. The health and virility of the nation was
embodied in that of the king. Thousands of years earlier,
when civilisation was beginning to develop in the Nile Valley,
the king reigned as long as his physical powers lasted. When
they began to fail he was probably sacrificed, a custom which
prevailed among other primitive peoples. With the passage
of time this custom was abandoned, but a relic of it survived
in what came to be called the *heb-sed* festival. At regular
intervals—originally every thirty-three years—the king
had to go through a ceremony in which he renewed his
health and vigour.[1] Part of this consisted in offering at the
altars of the gods of the Northern and Southern Kingdoms.
In the time of Djoser, for example (2800 B.C.), the King
had to run a fixed course, presumably to test his vitality,
and one of the most beautiful carved reliefs in Djoser's Step
Pyramid shows him performing this ritual sprint.

To the Ancient Egyptians, their king was not a human
being but a god, the son of Amun-Re himself. He never
died. He joined his father Amun; he "went to his horizon".
Take the description of the death of Amenemhat I in "The
Story of Sinuhe" quoted in Chapter X:

"King Amenemhat flew away to heaven and was united with
the son, and the god's body was merged with his creator. . . ."

Did the kings themselves believe that they were gods and
the sons of god? I believe that they did. One has only to
consider the effect of absolute power upon modern tyrants
and then add to that the sanction of religion, and the effect

---

[1] But later the ceremony was performed at shorter intervals.

of the sacramental atmosphere which surrounded the Egyptian kings from the cradle upwards, and it becomes impossible to believe otherwise.

The King was surrounded by ritual and symbolism. Every hour of his life was regulated by ceremony.

"Every hour was definitely allotted to various duties, to do something enjoined, and not to indulge in pleasures. On rising in the morning, the first thing was to read the despatches that had arrived, and this probably involved dictating the replies. Then came the ceremonial purification, the assumption of the robes and insignia, and proceeding to the sacrifice. Before that act the high priest, with the king and people standing around him, prayed for the health of the king, recited the praises of the king, and then a curse on all offences that had been ignorantly committed, laying the blame on the ministers. This must have been a considerable criticism of affairs, which, owing to the great power of the priesthood, would be hard to control officially; it is said that this was to guide and check the royal conduct. It is not stated whether the manual act of sacrifice was by the king or the high priest, but it was the king's ceremony, and he inspected the entrails. . . . He then finished the sacrifice, presumably the offerings of wine, oil, and other libations. Then followed the sermon, when the priests read edicts, laws and historical passages fitting for the time.

"The food of the kings is stated to have been plain and limited, which points to their being kept under regimen to preserve their health for the well-being of the country. In Africa, when a king shows weakening health, he is killed to prevent the country similarly suffering. It would appear that the Egyptian priesthood arose through the magician and the priest, and not from physical leadership. . . ."[1]

When State trials were held involving members of the Royal Family, they were held strictly according to legal form, without the king's presence. He had, in fact, less real power than the Emperor Claudius or King Henry VIII.

[1] Petrie, *Social Life in Ancient Egypt* (Constable).

Nor did his responsibilities end with the death of his
subjects. Just as in life he endowed them with land, so at
their death he endowed them for the future life land for
keeping up their tomb offerings. "Thus," says Petrie, "the
king was the maintenance of his people during life by his
vicarious position, and after death by his sustenance of them
in the tomb."

I have often wondered if the zest which Tuthmosis
showed for warfare, and his fondness for foreign campaigns,
may have been due in part to his desire to get away from
the cramping ritual of his office and express himself as a
human being in the way he understood best—as a general.

Look at him now, as he sits, weighed down by his heavy
crown, the royal cobra and falcon gleaming on his brow,
the crook and the flail held against his breast in the position
sanctioned by a tradition of more than 2,000 years.

"Life! Prosperity! Health!" shout the Pharaoh's people.
But as the bearers carry Tuthmosis on through the Hall of
Columns to the dark sanctuary where he, as High Priest,
must perform the sacred rites before Amun, he knows that
he is the people's Pharaoh.

*   *   *

The Pharaoh is offering sacrifice to the golden image of
Amun in the holiest part of the temple. Assisted by priests,
one wearing the mask of a hawk in impersonation of Horus,
the other in an ibis-headed mask of Thoth, the God of
Wisdom, he opens the door of the sacred shrine, fumigates
the statue with incense, sprinkles it with water from the
sacred lake, presents it with its crown and insignia, and sets
food offerings before it. The sanctuary is dimly lit by a small
aperture in the ceiling. The chanting of the priests sounds
faintly in the distance.

Meanwhile, like a glittering, many-coloured snake, a great
procession is coiling its way through the decorated streets of
Thebes, moving slowly towards the Temple. Dust rises from

the feet of columns of marching spearmen; other regiments follow: archers with long bows slung from the shoulders, quivers swinging at their sides; there are Nubians carrying clubs, foreign auxiliaries, Libyans, Shardana, bearded Syrians. Then come the chariots in a long, glittering line, the harnesses burnished, their horses adorned with nodding plumes of many colours. An endless, undulating roar goes up from the massed crowds as the soldiers march by. Ox-wagons follow, filled with booty, and columns of asses laden with the sack of cities, from Erkatu, from Tunip, from Kadesh, from Wawat; ornaments of gold and semi-precious stones; vessels of silver and gold; myrrh, incense wine, honey. Then come cattle, bulls, bull-calves, antelopes, gazelles, ibexes . . . and finally the human loot—hundreds of pitiful slaves, men and women, trudging along in the wake of the procession, and guarded by soldiers.

But the principal prisoners are not in the procession. Seven or eight kings and princes of the subjugated lands wait in an ante-chamber of the Temple, their clothes stained and ragged, their hands fast-pinioned behind their backs. Grim-faced Egyptian soldiers guard them, while outside the crowd waits for Pharaoh to emerge from the sanctuary. These men, according to a long-established custom, are to be sacrificed to Amun.

The procession has halted; officers move rapidly along the ranks, shouting orders and marshalling their men. All is ready for the moment when the Pharaoh leaves the Temple to mount his chariot of gold and electrum and to drive in triumph at the head of his victorious army.

One of the regiments of charioteers has drawn up near the entrance to the Temple. To it has been accorded the place of honour, for it has distinguished itself in battle. And in one of the chariots stand Senmut and Kenamun.

Senmut has recovered from his wounds, though they have left him with a permanent limp, and one side of his face is twisted. Bitterly he reflects that he has fought his last campaign. For Kenamun this should have been a moment of joy. He has been blooded in a tough campaign. He has seen action and acquitted himself well enough to earn promotion. But his pleasure is dimmed by sorrow for his friend.

"I wish they'd move," says Senmut, twisting the reins about his fingers and hitching at his belt.

"It's the moment of sacrifice," replies Kenamun.

"A barbarous custom," mutters Senmut, his face twitching.

"But it's the custom," objects Kenamun half-heartedly.

Senmut turns on him savagely.

"There you speak like your father," he says. "It is the *custom*. Always in Egypt it is the *custom*. So our fathers did and so must we do."

"But the Asiatics would have done the same to us."

"Is that any reason why we should imitate the barbarians?"

Kenamun sighs, and then says: "It seems you don't like Egypt."

"You are wrong," replies his friend. "I do like Egypt. But is that any reason why I should approve everything that's done here? Not all the foreigners sacrifice their noble prisoners. The Keftiu do not."

"But they do, Senmut. Paibese told me that they sacrifice their prisoners to their god, a bull."

"Then Paibese is a fool. He means the bull-leaping, which is not the same thing."

"The bull-leaping?"

"Yes. The Keftiu train their prisoners to encounter the bull in the arena. They have to leap over its horns. But if they are brave and skilful they can escape death. That is not the same as dashing out your prisoner's brains with a club. . . ."

A great and terrible roar comes from the direction of the temple. It is taken up by the crowd and spreads far and wide through the city. Senmut shudders. "It's over," he says. "Now perhaps we can move."

In the Hall of Columns the bodies of the slain chieftans lie in a pool of blood. Nofret and the priestesses shake their *systra*, and begin the Battle Hymn of Amun. Their thin, high voices echo from the lofty roof, mingling with those of the priests:

"I have come, causing thee to smite the princes of Zahi;

I have hurled them beneath thy feet among the highlands.

I have caused them to see thy majesty as lord of radiance,

So that thou hast shone in their faces like my image.

I have come, causing thee to smite the Asiatics,

Thou hast made captive the heads of the Asiatics of Retenu.

I have caused them to see thy majesty equipped with thy adornment,

When thou takest the weapons of war in the chariot. . . ."

Slowly the King is borne from the Temple on the shoulders of his bearers. The massed crowds prostrate themselves again as he mounts his war chariot and moves to the head of his waiting troops. Then, amid the shrilling of pipes, the clashing of tambourines, and the beat of drums, it begins to move.

Senmut jerks the reins.

"I'd like to go to Keftiu-land," he says.

HOUSE OF ETERNITY

AUTUMN has come, and with it the Inundation. Far, far to the south, the waters of the Blue Nile, swollen by rains, are rushing into the main stream, bearing a rich treasure of fertilising mud from the mountains of Abyssinia. But the Ancient Egyptians have never heard of Abyssinia, or the Blue Nile. For them the world ends south of Nubia, and the life-giving flood, the yearly miracle, comes as the gift of Re. At Thebes and other towns along the serpentine length of the river, the priests are studying the "Nilometers", measuring the level of the flood-water and comparing it with those of previous years. It is a "good Nile" this year, and already scribes are calculating the expected yield of the land, and the amount of taxation which can be levied. The river began to rise three months ago, in August, when the Egyptians held the High Nile Festival. Last month, September, it was at its highest. Now it is October, and in a few weeks it will begin to subside, and sowing will commence in November.

A strange stillness broods over the imperial city. Where, a few months ago, there were green fields stretching to the foot of the limestone hills there is now a lake-like expanse of water. You can take a boat from the quayside on the eastern bank and land within a short distance of the Necropolis on the western side. Many of the peasants are idle, but some have been recruited for work on the monuments. Big boats are arriving from distant Assuan loaded with granite, and in the Temple of Karnak work is being done on the reconstruction and extension of the Temple. Gangs of sweating men haul on ropes, grunting a rhythmic chorus as a 600-ton obelisk is slowly raised into position.

It is early morning. Boats move continually across the broad, brown river, their sails throwing long shadows which point towards the western cliffs. The voices of the boatmen come clearly across the water, and somewhere a pipe plays plaintively.

In one of the boats, a big, handsome craft with gilt mountings, sit Rekhmire and his wife, Meryet. They are going to visit Rekhmire's tomb, his "House of Eternity", which has been hewn out of the western cliffs in preparation for the Vizier's death. There is nothing unusual in this. Men of rank spent as much time and care on the preparation of their eternal homes as they did on their earthly dwellings, for life is short and death is long. And "home" is a much more accurate description than "tomb", because the Egyptian planned his sepulchre as the everlasting dwelling-place of his *ka* or spirit.

These tombs vary in size according to the wealth and importance of their owner, but they have certain features in common. There is a deep shaft leading to the sealed burial-chamber, in which lies the embalmed body. There is a chamber containing the statues of the deceased and usually his wife, facing the offering-chamber or chapel in which the relatives of the dead noble make food-offerings for his spirit. The statue, which accurately represents the dead man as he appeared in life, is intended as a dwelling-place of the spirit when it leaves the body to partake of the offerings. The walls of these chambers, as described in an earlier chapter, are covered with paintings or sculptured reliefs representing the activities of the dead man in life, which he wishes should continue in the after-life. There are also sacred texts to assist him when he appears in the Judgement Hall of Osiris, and representations of his relatives making their offerings, which by a process of sympathetic magic will become real should his descendants fail in their duty.

The boat glides to the landing stage. The Vizier and his

wife disembark; servants assist them into carrying-chairs, and in these they are carried up the slope towards the cliff-face. On their way they pass through the many-streeted town in which live the embalmers, the coffin-makers, the carvers and painters, the makers of funerary furniture, and the priests whose duty is to make regular offerings at the tombs. Through one open doorway they see gilt and painted coffins leaning against a wall. This is a coffin-maker's showroom, in which relatives of the dead may choose the design which best pleases them. Within are also tables set out with miniature mummy-cases which serve the same purpose. Nearby are the embalmer's booths, temporary structures which are erected for each person to be embalmed, and dismantled afterwards when the work is complete. From one booth comes the strong smell of natron from the natron-baths in which the bodies are soaked for the requisite number of days.

It takes seventy days to complete the full process of embalmment and mummification, but there are quicker and cheaper methods. In fact, the embalmers will offer you a choice of three alternative processes, according to how much you wish to pay. The most expensive method is as follows:

"First they draw out the brain through the nostrils with an iron hook, taking part of it out this way, the rest by pouring in drugs. Next, with a sharp Ethiopian stone, they make an incision in the flank, and take out the entrails, and after cleansing the body and scouring it with palm-wine, they purify it with pounded incense; then, having filled the body with pure pounded myrrh and cassia and other perfumes—frankincense excepted—they sew it up again. Having done this they soak the body in natron, keeping it covered for seventy days, for it is not lawful to soak it for a longer time than this. And when the seventy days are accomplished they wash the corpse, and wrap the whole body in fine linen cut into strips, smearing it with gum, which the Egyptians use instead of glue. After this the relatives, having taken the corpse back again, make a wooden case of human shape, and, having made it, place the corpse inside and, having closed it up, put it in a sepulchral chamber. . . .

"For those who desire the medium style to avoid heavy expense, they prepare the corpse thus: Having charged their syringes with cedar oil, they fill the inside of the corpse without making any incision or removing the viscera, but inject it at the anus. Then they close the aperture to prevent the liquid from escaping and soak the body in natron for the prescribed number of days. On the last day they let out the cedar oil which had been previously injected, and such is its potency that it brings away the bowels and internal parts in a fluid state, and the natron dissolves the flesh so that nothing remains but the skin and bones. When this has been done, they return the body without further manipulation.

"The third manner of embalming is this, which is used only for persons of slender means: After washing out the body with a purgative they soak it in natron for seventy days and deliver it to be taken back."

That was how Herodotus described the process in the 5th century B.C., but the methods were traditional and had been in use for thousands of years. The bodies of men and women of the Eighteenth Dynasty were embalmed in a similar manner.

As Rekhmire and Meryet mount the slope towards the tombs in the cliff-side, they stop to allow a cortége to pass them. First come servants carrying alabaster jars containing food and precious unguents; then come men carrying long wooden chests containing the ornaments and clothes of the dead man. A sled follows, dragged by two men; inside are the canopic jars containing the embalmed viscera which have been removed from the body. Before it strides a lector-priest, chanting solemnly. Other priests accompany the body itself, the mummy resting on a couch beneath a canopy, the whole mounted on another sled.

"In peace, in peace, unto the Great God," cry the priests as the procession passes. Behind them come the family and their friends, and a group of professional women mourners, who weep and tear their hair, beating their breasts and sending up the old wailing cry for the dead.

The Vizier and his wife watch the cortége as it passes out of sight round a projecting bastion of rock; then they signal to the carriers, who lift the chairs and carry them up the steep path to the tomb-entrance.

In front is a courtyard 60 feet wide; behind it the cliff-side has been smoothed flat, forming an imposing façade to the tomb, the tall entrance to which is exactly in the centre. The foreman of the workmen comes to greet his lord, falling on his knees and touching the ground with his forehead. Then he rises and stands respectfully on one side as the nobleman and his wife pass through the entrance. As it is early morning, the sun streams directly through the doorway and lights up the interior, so that the hundreds of figures which seem to march along the plastered walls, the reddish-brown skins of the men, the pale cream complexions of the women, the white robes, the gold of their ornaments, the blue, green, and red of their jewels seem to glow with an unearthly light.

To help the illusion, the foreman has caused bronze mirrors to be placed at an angle to right and left of the entrance, so that not only is the east-west passage opposite the entrance illuminated by the direct rays of the sun, but the transverse passage which opens out to right and left is also lit by reflected light.

The tomb is, in fact, T-shaped, the cross-bar of the T running parallel with the face of the cliff, the long arm of the T stretching from the entrance for more than 100 feet into the hill. This narrow passage is like a funnel, relatively low at the entrance, but the roof slopes upwards at a fairly steep angle till it reaches the far wall at a considerable height above the entrance. And high on that wall, just below the painted ceiling, is a niche, within which rest life-like statues of Rekhmire and Meryet, seated, with Meryet's arm placed affectionately around her husband's waist. The effect is startling, particularly at this moment when the sunlight streams full on to the figures.

At the far end of the hall workmen perched on scaffolding are applying colour to the designs which the draughtsmen have left. Others are carefully painting in the hieroglyphic texts which describe the scenes. While Meryet is critically regarding her statue, her husband is examining the texts on the south side of the wall beneath, which describe his appointment as Vizier. There sits Tuthmosis, wearing his tall crown and clad in the cerements of Osiris. In front of him stands Rekhmire, with his titles above him. The text reads:

"The guiding principles enjoined on the Vizier Rekhmire; the assembling of the council at the audience hall of Pharaoh—life, prosperity, and health to him!—and causing the newly appointed Vizier to be brought in.

"His Majesty said to him, 'Look thou to the hall of the Vizier and be vigilant over all the procedure in it. Lo, it is the consolidation of the entire land. Lo, as to [the position of a] vizier, lo, it is not pleasant at all; no, it is bitter as gall. [Lo] it is the bronze which surrounds the gold of the house of its [lord]. Lo it is to have no consideration for himself or for the officials of the magistracy, and not to make slaves of the general public. Lo, as to all that a man does in the house of his lord he speaks approvingly. Lo, what he does is not . . . for any other man.

" 'Lo, if a petitioner of Upper or Lower Egypt, [that is] the entire land, come, prepared for the court . . . to hear [his case] thou shalt see well to it that all the procedure is in accord with what has legal sanction, that all the procedure is in accord with due regularity. . . .

" 'Lo, whenever an administrator hears cases let there be publicity, and let water and air report about all that he may do. Lo, then, his conduct is by no means unperceived. If he does anything [unseemly] and he is to blame he is not to be reinstalled on the authority of an acting official but men shall learn of it on the authority of his [proper] judge. . . .' "

Meryet, bored by the long text which her husband has begun to read, has wandered into one of the transverse rooms. Here the workmen are just putting the finishing touches on a scene depicting a family feast. There sit Rekhmire and Meryet, larger than life-size, with their guests. A little band of musicians plays, and the words of their song is set down beside them:

"[Put] balsam on the locks of Ma'et, for health and life are with her . . . ! O Amun, the heaven is uplifted for thee; the ground is trodden for thee; Ptah with his two hands makes a chapel as a resting place for thy heart. Come, O north wind! I saw thee when I was on the tower."

In another scene, two women and two young girls, the daughters of Rekhmire, hold out to him the systra, which he touches. The text says:

"The enjoyment of the sight of good food, music, dancing, and song, anointment with oil of balsam and unction with olive oil, lotus held to the nostril, bread, beer, date wine, and dainties of all sorts, presented to the *ka* of the seigneur, mayor of the city, Rekhmire, his heartily loved wife, mistress of his house, Meryet, being with him."[1]

In a lower picture one of Rekhmire's sons, Amenhotep, and two of his brothers, offer flowers, saying:

"Enjoyment, glad exultation, and participation in good food, summer lotus for the nostril, and [oil of] balsam suitable for the crown of the head, for the *ka* of the seigneur, mayor of the city, and Vizier, Rekhmire, and his wife, Meryet."

The graceful young girls place flimsy collars round the necks of the ladies, and pour wine or beer into their cups with the murmur:

"For thy *ka*! Spend a festive day!"

[1] See illustration opposite p. 192.

And a group of three women, who are beating time to the music while they accept drink and ointment, remark:

"Can it be Ma'et in whose face there is a desire for deep drinking?"

Then Meryet is joined by her husband, who leads her to another part of the passage to admire a scene which depicts him inspecting the temple workshops of Amun. There are the jewellers drilling beads, the makers of alabaster vases, the carpenters making inlaid wooden cabinets, the leather-workers, the rope-makers, the sandal-makers. And there too, much larger than his workmen, is the Vizier himself leaning on his staff with his train of forty retainers.

"This noble, who lays down principles and guides the hands of his workmen, making furniture of ivory and ebony, *ssndm* wood, *mrw* wood, and true cedar from the summit of the mountain slopes of Lebanon."

There are the metal-workers also casting the bronze doors for the Temple of Amun. The artist has just finished this scene, and looks to the Vizier for his approval. Rekhmire is satisfied, not only with the picture, but with the accompanying text, which reads:

"Bringing Asiatic copper which His Majesty carried off from his victory in the land of Retenu, in order to cast the two doors of the Temple of Amun at Karnak, overlaid with gold which gleams (?) like the horizon of heaven. It was the Mayor and Vizier Rekhmire who directed it."

Now the couple return to the main hall, where the statues stand. On the north end wall is the Vizier's family history, with the names of his uncle, Woser, who was also a Vizier, and other ancestors. Here Rekhmire and Meryet are shown seated at table, while their son Menkheperre-Sonb, "Scribe of the temple dues of Amun", dressed in a leopard-skin is consecrating their food. Another son, Amenhotep, is there too; Kenamun is not shown, though he appears in another picture. But three of the daughters are there, Ta-kha'et, Mut-Nofret, and Henet-towy.

Opposite, covering the length and breadth of the south wall, is an enormous inscription describing in full detail the appointment of Rekhmire to the Vizierate: he is careful to flatter the King.

"When a second day had dawned and the morrow was come, I was summoned again into the presence of the good god, Menkhe-perre—may he live for ever—even Horus, the victorious bull appearing gloriously in Thebes. Now His Majesty knows what happens; there is nothing at all of which he is ignorant. He is Thoth in every respect. There is no matter that he has ever failed to discern. Every affair . . . he is cognisant of it like the Great Lady of writing. He changes the design into its execution like the god who ordains and performs.

"So His Majesty opened his mouth and spake his words before me: 'Behold, my eyes send me to my heart [for as much as My Majesty] knows the decisions are many and there is no end to them, and the judgement of cases never flags. Mayest thou act according as I say; then will Ma'et rest in her place.' He ad-monished me very greatly: 'Armour thyself; be strong in action; weary not; accuse evil. . . .' "

Then follow thousands of words of what seems to us like self-appraisement; but we should do the Vizier an injustice if we accused him of mere vanity. He has his share of it, like most men who have reached great eminence, but now, in his tomb-inscriptions, he is not boasting before men, but trying desperately to justify himself before the gods of the Underworld:

"I judged [poor and] rich alike. I rescued the weak from the [passionate] moment of the infuriated. I restrained weeping by replacing [it with] an avenger. I defended the husbandless widow. I established the son and heir on the seat of his father. I relieved the old man, giving him my staff, and causing the old women to say, 'What a good action.' . . ."

Meryet takes her husband's arm affectionately. The sun is rising, the tomb is becoming hot and stuffy, and she wishes to leave. But the Vizier lingers for a few more moments to study a painting which shows him receiving the tribute of the foreigners.

Here is a procession of Asiatics, men from Retenu whom Tuthmosis has vanquished. The porters carry—and the inscriptions describe—ingots of copper, jars of olive oil, gold and silver rings, lead, timber, chariots, and horses.

"The arrival in peace of the chiefs of Retenu and all the lands of Further Asia in deferential obeisance," runs the text, "their tribute on their back, in the hope that there would be given to them the breath of life because of loyalty to His Majesty; for they have seen his great victories—yea, his terribleness has dominated their hearts.

"Now it was the father and favourite of the god, the confidant of the King, the Mayor of the city, the Vizier Rekhmire, who received the tribute of the various lands. . . ."

There are men from Punt, men from Nubia, and men from Crete (Keftiu-land) and the islands of the Mediterranean. The Vizier and his wife look curiously at the paintings of the curling-haired, slim-waisted men of proud bearing, carrying the rich and lovely products of their country—the gold and silver vases, the tapering gold cups, elaborately wrought, the bulls' heads in gold, the richly-ornamented arms which were more beautiful than the products of Asia.[1] Rekhmire has met their ambassadors, and he knows that they come as friendly traders, as representatives of a free and equal state, unlike the men of Pharaoh's dominions. Still—

"It was the confidant of the sovereign, the mayor and Vizier Rekhmire, who received the tribute. . . ."

Glancing down from the figures, Meryet says: "I wonder where Senmut is. . . ."

[1] See illustration opposite p. 192.

"He should be passing the Delta by now," replies her husband, leading her from the tomb.

For Senmut, through the influence of Rekhmire, has been sent on an Embassy to the far-off island which few Egyptians have ever seen. The restless young officer, unable any longer to gratify his lust for travel by warfaring in Syria, has found another outlet. He is on his way to Keftiu-land, and perhaps Egypt may never see him again.

The sunlight stabs their eyes as they leave the tomb. They seat themselves in their carrying-chairs and are carried down the path, past the city of the workmen, and so to the riverside. As they climb into their barge again, Rekhmire looks at the bank and notices the water-mark left by the subsiding river. He nods towards it and remarks to Meryet: "It's beginning to go down." The tackle creaks, the sail spreads lazily in the slight breeze as the boat moves back across the Nile towards Thebes. The Vizier settles himself under his awning and looks across the dazzling water towards the city.

So it all begins again. Soon the fields will be uncovered, and the sowers will be moving across the black mud, singing as they scatter the grain. Then the black expanse will give way to a haze of green, and before long the reapers will be out with their curved sickles, harvesting the crops. He had seen it all so many times. He had shown it in his tomb:

"Rekhmire . . . born of Bet and begotten of the *w'b* priest of Amun, Nefer-weben, son of the Mayor and Vizier, Amotu, enjoying the sight of the cows, delighting in the work of the fields and beholding the work of the seasons, summer and winter. . . ."

And the servants cry:

"Accept the good produce . . . and eat, O Mayor and Vizier, a happy beginning, a happy day, a happy year, free from evil. . . ."

"Son of Nefer-weben. . . ." His father had been only a

humble priest of Amun when he, Rekhmire, was born. Could the old man have been a prophet and seen his son's great destiny when he named him Rekh-mi-Re—"Wise as God"? It was a pleasing thought. Yes, the gods had been good to him.

Yet greatness had brought its cares. "Lo, the position of a Vizier, lo, it is not pleasant at all." . . . An exaggeration, of course, but there were times when he felt a slight nostalgia for his carefree youth, when, like Senmut, he had travelled abroad as a youthful official. Senmut . . . he wondered how he would fare in the land of the Keftiu? He, Rekhmire, would like to have seen it, but it was too late now.

As for the future, who could tell? He still hoped for many years of life, but the king was old, and when he went to his horizon, and a new king took his place, who knew what might happen? There had been more than one instance of great officials who had fallen from their high office when a new king sat on the throne of Pharaoh. But that was for the gods to decide.

His arm stole around the shoulders of his wife. Yes, life had been good. He had had many children, and seen some of them rise high in the favour of the King. His tomb was prepared, and every provision made for his welfare in the life to come. He had served the King well, and the King knew his worth:

"He saw to it that the chapel of my tomb should last me for ever. He saw to it that my name should be stable therein, lasting and secure for millions of years, and that my memory should be lasting therein for ever and ever."

FACT OR FICTION?

W HEN I began to write this book I had no definite idea of what form it would finally take. My purpose was to depict as vividly and realistically as I could the daily life of the Ancient Egyptians, in the following order: their religion; their administrative system; the houses they lived in; their pastimes and recreations; the status of their womenfolk; with chapters dealing with education, the life of the labourers and craftsmen, the professions of soldier, doctor, and lawyer; literature, and the function of the Pharaoh in relation to his people. And in order to avoid producing a mere catalogue of facts, I decided to present this material in a semi-fictitious framework, although I knew that this method, though attractive, was difficult and a little dangerous, in that it might lay me open to the criticism that I was not presenting history, but fantasy.

Therefore, I would like to assure readers who have read this book mainly for informing them, that the bulk of the material is completely factual, and that where I have invented scenes and characters they are based almost entirely on known and recorded incidents. To reassure them still further, I will now separate the facts from the "imaginative reconstruction".

Rekhmire was a real person. So was his wife, Meryet, his daughters, Mut-Nofret and Ta'kha'et, and his sons, Menkheperre-Sonb, Amenhotep, and Mer-y. All their names are given in the tomb, together with that of Kenamun, though archaeologists are uncertain whether the latter was a son or grandson. The first-named three sons were priests or officials, but Kenamun's occupation is not given, which is why I made him a soldier.

All that is known of Rekhmire is contained in his tomb-inscriptions, which describe in great detail his functions as a great administrator. Nothing of his domestic and social life is known save that he gave banquets and parties, which are illustrated and described in his tomb, as in those of other Egyptian officials.

Apart from the voyage described in Chapter II and Rekhmire's visit to the Tomb in Chapter XIII, every incident I have described in the life of the Vizier is based on his tomb-inscriptions. Nothing is known of the lives of Mut-Nofret, Ta'kha'et, and Kenamun, but all the incidents in which I have involved them could have happened. To take a few examples; Nozme getting drunk at the party—there are several illustrations of drunken female guests in the tombs, including one being overcome by the final stages of nausea;[1] Ta'kha'et's garden party is based entirely on the love-poem, "The Trees in the Garden"; the hunting-party at which Senut and Kenamun are present is based on tomb-paintings and descriptions; the boy Per-hor is imaginary, but young sons of the nobility did attend schools attached to the temples, and the school exercises are contemporary. Kenamun's adventures in Syria are fictitious, but based on contemporary documents describing the Pharaoh's Asiatic campaigns. The officer Amenemhab, who arranged for Kenamun to go to Syria, was a real person. His tomb can be seen in the Theban Necropolis, in which he describes the deeds of valour which he performed. He claims to have been first into the breach at the taking of Kadesh in year 42 of Tuthmosis's reign. He was a favourite of Tuthmosis III and his wife was the royal nurse.

The young man Sinuhe, the lover of Ta'kha'et, is fictitious; so is Senmut, but the details of his military

[1] One guest is recorded as saying, "Behold I wish to drink until I am drunk. My inside is like a straw!"

career are taken from those of other officers. Even his appointment as ambassador is not improbable. There is a record of an officer of chariotry who later represented his country at a foreign court. Some readers may object that the views he expresses are out of harmony with conventional Egyptian ideas. To this I can only reply that history is not wanting in examples of young men who were ahead of their time; I can point to the Pharaoh Akhnaten, who, only a short while after the life of my hero, began a religious and aesthetic revolution, abolishing at one sweep the worship of Amun and hundreds of lesser gods, and substituting the veneration of one deity—the "Aten". He also seems to have been strongly influenced by Crete—the "land of the Keftiu"—to judge from the art which he encouraged.

Nofret's role of priestess is highly probable. It was customary for the daughters of the nobility to perform this office; the Queen herself sometimes acted as High Priestess, the "Bride of Amun". Her illness, too, is credible, and as for the "cure" there are many examples in the medical papyri of charms and spells to drive away fever. There is one which runs:

"Run thou out, O disease! Son of a disease! Who breakest down the bones, destroyeth the skull, disturbest the brain, and dost cause to ache the seven openings in the heads of the Followers of Horus, who turn to Thoth! Behold, I have brought the remedy against thee, the potion against thee, even the milk of one who has borne a boy, and odorous gum! May it force thee out! May it force thee out! May it drive thee forth! Come forth upon the ground! Rot! Rot! Rot! Rot!"[1]

In this case a drug is indicated, but often charms only were used.

The wars of Tuthmosis III are well-documented in the *Annals*, and the triumphal processions to the Temple of

[1] Shorter, *Everyday Life in Ancient Egypt.*

Amun are depicted on the temple walls. In the same inscriptions, the King is shown personally dashing out the brains of captive chiefs with a club. There is some doubt as to this act being real or symbolic. At some period of Egyptian history it was certainly real. Equally barbarous acts are depicted on inscriptions of a later period than that of Tuthmosis III. For example, one of the Rameses is shown returning in triumph to Thebes with seven Syrian chiefs hung head downward from the prow of his ship. I have assumed that such sacrifices were still made in the time of the Warrior-King Tuthmosis III, though whether the King himself performed them is open to doubt.

At the same time, the Egyptians were not as cruel as the Assyrians and other Oriental peoples. For example, the customs of killing the servants of a king and burying them in his tomb was abandoned early in Egyptian history, *shawabti*-figures statuettes being substituted. The ritual killing of the king when he became unfit to rule was also replaced by the *heb-sed* ceremony; and there are other examples. These, and the humane laws set down in the tomb of Rekhmire, incline me to believe that men of Senmut's character were not unknown in Ancient Egypt, and that therefore his protest against such a barbaric survival is credible.

Readers may like to know what happened to Rekhmire in his later years. A little is known. He survived Tuthmosis III, living on into the reign of his successor, Amenophis II. There is a scene in the tomb showing the Vizier making a voyage down the river to meet the young King, who was returning to Thebes when his father died, after a reign of fifty-four years. The scenes continue with the succession of Amenophis II, and then come to a sudden end, suggesting a tragic close.

Whether or not the Vizier fell from office during the lifetime of the new Pharaoh is not known, but it may well have happened. Throughout the tomb a systematic attempt has been made to obliterate his name and the figures of himself and his wife wherever the spoilers could reach them. This was the usual fate of an Egyptian tomb when its owners' enemies triumphed. His body has not been found. Mr. de Garis Davies, whose beautiful volumes, *The Tomb of Rekhmire at Thebes*, should be read by all who are interested in this period of Egyptian history, writes:

"In the corner of the court near the left end of the façade there is a small burial-shaft (which may or may not be contemporary) giving access to a chamber to the south. Six other burial shafts have been sunk within the tomb; but none of them has yielded any trace of burial furniture belonging to the original occupants. Either, then, the place of interment of Rekhmire is still undiscovered, or exceptional care was taken to destroy every aid to his survival into eternity, even the protection of the gods in their temples, where he must have left memorials, being refused him. Such bitter malice seems unlikely when one notices how incomplete was the destruction of his memory on the walls of the tomb. Apparently burial in Thebes was denied him; perhaps he was exiled to some remote part of Egypt and interred there."[1]

But in spite of the mutilations and the neglect and damage which the tomb has suffered in 3,000 years, it is perhaps the most impressive and interesting example of a nobleman's tomb of the New Kingdom. When I revisited it in 1953 and saw the fine work of restoration and cleaning done by the Egyptian Government's Antiquities Department, I resolved to make the Vizier the central character of my book. I hope I have not done him an injustice.

May I say respectfully to his *ka*: "Now let thy heart be glad, O noble, and all thy affairs be fortunate!"

[1] Egyptian Expedition publications, Metropolitan Museum of Art, New York.

ACKNOWLEDGMENTS

The author and publishers are indebted to the following for quotations made in this book:

Constable & Co. Ltd. for the extracts from Petrie's *Social Life in Ancient Egypt*; J. M. Dent & Sons Ltd. for the extracts from the Everyman Edition of *History* by Herodotus; Egypt Exploration Society for the quotations from R. O. Faulkner's article *Egyptian Military Organisation*; Fouad University Press for the quotations from the writings of Dr. P. C. Sobhy Bey; Macmillan & Co. Ltd. for the extracts from Erman's *Life in Ancient Egypt*; Methuen & Co. Ltd. for the extracts from Erman's *The Literature of Ancient Egypt*; The Metropolitan Museum of Art for the quotation from *The Tomb of Rekh-mi-Re*; The Clarendon Press for the extracts from *The Legacy of Egypt*; Sampson Low, Marston Co. Ltd. for the extract from *Everyday Life in Ancient Egypt*, by A. W. Shorter; Sidgwick and Jackson for the quotation from Margaret Murray's *The Splendour that was Egypt*; The University of Chicago Press for the quotation from *The Intellectual Adventure of Ancient Man*, by Frankfort, Wilson and Jacobsen, published in Great Britain under the title, *Before Philosophy*.

THE DYNASTIES OF ANCIENT EGYPT

First and Second Dynasties . . . *c.* 3200–2780 B.C.
   In 3200 B.C. Menes combined in unity for the first time
the Kingdoms of Upper and Lower Egypt.

OLD KINGDOM, 2780–2100 B.C.

Third Dynasty . . . . 2780–2720 B.C.
Fourth Dynasty . . . . 2720–2560 B.C.
Fifth Dynasty . . . . . 2560–2420 B.C.
Sixth Dynasty . . . . . 2420–2270 B.C.
Seventh to Tenth Dynasties (First Inter-
   mediate Period) . . . . 2270–2100 B.C.

THE MIDDLE EMPIRE, 2100–1700 B.C.

Eleventh Dynasty . . . . 2100–2000 B.C.
Twelfth Dynasty . . . . 2000–1790 B.C.
Thirteenth Dynasty . . . . 1790–1700 B.C.

HYKSOS PERIOD, *c.* 1700–1555 B.C.

Fourteenth to Sixteenth Dynasties *c.* 1700–1600 B.C.
Seventeenth Dynasty . . . . 1600–1555 B.C.

NEW EMPIRE, 1555–712 B.C.

Eighteenth Dynasty . . . . 1555–1350 B.C.
Nineteenth Dynasty . . . . 1350–1200 B.C.
Twentieth Dynasty . . . . 1200–1090 B.C.
Twenty-first Dynasty (Tanites) . . 1090–945 B.C.
Twenty-second Dynasty . . . 945–745 B.C.
Twenty-third Dynasty . . . 745–718 B.C.
Twenty-fourth Dynasty . . . 718–712 B.C.

LATE EGYPTIAN PERIOD, 712–525 B.C.

Twenty-fifth Dynasty .   .   .   .   712–663 B.C.
Twenty-sixth Dynasty   .   .   .   663–525 B.C.

PERSIAN DOMINATION, 525–332 B.C.

Twenty-seventh Dynasty   .   .   .   525–338 B.C.
Twenty-eighth Dynasty   .   .   .   404–339 B.C.
Twenty-ninth Dynasty   .   .   .   398–379 B.C.
Thirtieth Dynasty   .   .   .   .   378–332 B.C.

GRAECO–ROMAN PERIOD

(1) Alexander the Great and Ptolemies   332–30 B.C.
(2) Roman Period   .   .   .   .   30 B.C.–A.D. 395
(3) Byzantine Period   .   .   .   A.D. 395–638

BIBLIOGRAPHY

Baikie, J., *Egyptian Antiquities in the Nile Valley* (Methuen).

Bouquet, *Comparative Religion* (Penguin Books).

Breasted, J. H., *Ancient Records of Egypt* (University of Chicago Press).

Breasted, J. H., *History of Egypt* (Hodder and Stoughton).

Breasted, J. H., *The Development of Religion and Thought in Ancient Egypt*.

Budge, W., *The Literature of the Egyptians* (Methuen).

Clarke, S. and Engelbach, R., *Ancient Egyptian Masonry* (Oxford, 1930).

Cottrell, L., *The Lost Pharaohs* (Evans).

Cottrell, L., *The Bull of Minos* (Evans).

Davies, N. de Garis, *The Tomb of Rekhmire at Thebes* (Egyptian Expedition Publications, Metropolitan Museum of Art, New York).

Driotron and Lauer, *Sakkarah: the Monuments of Zoser* (Institut de l'Archiologie Orientale).

Edwards, J. E. S., *The Pyramids of Egypt* (Penguin Books).

Elliot-Smith and Dawson, *Egyptian Mummies* (George Allen and Unwin).

Engelbach, R., *Mechanical and Technical Processes*. Chapter 5, "The Legacy of Egypt" (Oxford, Clarendon Press, 1952)

Erman and Blackman, *The Literature of the Ancient Egyptians* (Methuen).

Erman, A., *Life in Ancient Egypt* (Macmillan).

Erman, A., *A Handbook of Egyptian Religion* (London, 1907).

Evans, Sir A., *The Palace of Minos* (Macmillan).

Faulkner, "Egyptian Military Organisation", *Journal of Egyptian Archaeology*, Vol. 39.

Frankfort, Wilson and Jacobsen, *Before Philosophy* (Penguin Books).

Gardiner, Sir A., *Topographical Catalogue of the Private Tombs of Thebes* (Quaritch).

Gardiner, Sir A., *The Chester Beatty Papyrus*.

Gardiner, A. H., *The Attitude of the Ancient Egyptians to Death and the Dead.* (Cambridge, 1935).

Glanville, S. R. K., (Editor), *The Legacy of Egypt* (Clarendon Press).

Herodotus, *History* (translated Rawlinson) (Dent).

Lucas, A., *Ancient Egyptian Materials and Industries*. Second edition (London, 1934).

Mercer, S., *The Religion of Ancient Egypt* (London, Luzac and Co., 1949).

Murray, Dr. M., *The Splendour that was Egypt* (Sidgwick and Jackson).

Petrie, W. M. F., *Social Life in Ancient Egypt* (Constable).

Petrie, W. M. F., *The Building of a Pyramid in Ancient Egypt* (1930, Part II, London).

Shorter, *Everyday Life in Ancient Egypt* (Sampson Low and Marston).

Sobhy, Dr., *Lectures in the History of Medicine* (Fouad University Press, Cairo).

Weigall, A., *The Glory of the Pharaohs* (Thornton Butterworth).

INDEX